MODERN
CANDY
CONTAINERS
& NOVELTIES

Identification
& Value Guide

Jack Brush
&
William Miller

COLLECTOR BOOKS
A Division of Schroeder Publishing Co., Inc.

The current values in this book should be used only as a guide. They are not intended to set prices, which vary from one section of the country to another. Auction prices as well as dealer prices vary greatly and are affected by condition and demand. Neither the authors nor the publisher assumes responsibility for any losses which might be incurred as a result of consulting this guide.

Cover design: Beth Summers
Book design: Mary Ann Hudson

Searching For A Publisher?

We are always looking for knowledgeable people considered experts within their fields. If you feel that there is a real need for a book on your collectible subject and have a large comprehensive collection, contact Collector Books.

Collector Books
P.O. Box 3009
Paducah, KY 42002-3009
www.collectorbooks.com

✳ Contents ✳

Introduction

This book is not a complete list of candy containers. It provides over 500 pictures and descriptions of recent containers with a price guide.

"Crossover collectibles," as defined by *Iron Talk's* May/June 1996 issue, are collectibles of interest to more than one specialty group. What is *Iron Talk? Iron Talk* is a journal of antique pressing irons and that is about as specialized as you can get. Featured in the mentioned article are candy containers in the shape of pressing irons. As mentioned in the article crossover collectibles have an elevated premium. We see that in candy containers as the most popular and valuable containers are cross collectibles in popular specialties i.e.: Batman, Santa, etc.

Sometime in December, just before Christmas, I was shopping and spotted a little Santa Claus with candy in it. I just could not resist it. It reminded me of the day when I was a small boy, and received a glass toy. It too had candy in it. Toys were hard to come by in those days. After World War II, things got better. All the materials were not being used in the war effort any more. The 5 & 10 cent store was able to get a greater variety of things. Things for me in those days were *toys*. Plastic was starting to show up little by little. Today most of the toys are made of plastic, and when I saw that Santa Claus I had to have him. Well a lot of Decembers have come and gone, and I have fallen in love with the candy containers of today.

The best part of it is, it's *fun*! These little toys are made with a lot of detail, color, and thought. You don't have to be a millionaire or an Einstein to collect or enjoy today's candy containers.

The next time you are in a store, go to the candy counter, shelf, or wherever they keep their candy, and see if they have any. Check them out. They're great. All us kids like them.

J.P. Brush

Past experience with collecting has proven the value of a reference book, which helps in so many ways. Is it the real thing? When did they make it? What is the value of my collectible? All these and many more questions can be answered only by years of collecting, making mistakes, and talking to people who know, or you can save a lot of time, money, and heartache and get yourself a good book on the collectible you are trying to find.

This book has photos, descriptions, and history of modern day plastic candy containers. The more you know about candy containers, the better you can buy, sell, and trade them. The value of a collectible is what someone is willing to pay for it. One day it is worth $1.00 and another day it might double or triple. Collect what you enjoy. Candy containers are colorful and nostalgic. They are small (don't take up much room), low cost, and fun. If they follow the glass candy containers of the past, they can end up being very profitable.

First and foremost, collecting is fun. Profit is secondary, but it is still there. With all the photos (one picture is worth a thousand words) and thousands of words written about these candy containers, you are on your way to becoming an expert in the brand new field of plastic candy containers.

It features many of the popular characters, such as Batman, Spiderman, The Hulk, Bugs Bunny, Porky Pig, Snoopy, Tweety, and many, many more.

4

History of Candy Containers

Generation after generation, candy novelties have delighted children. Today's sophisticated, interactive breed that "talks, plays music, or spins," is a distant cousin to the original hot sellers: glass figural filled with pressed candy. While more accurately described as candy containers than candy-filled toys, they still managed to capture the imaginations of kids more than a century ago, becoming popular playthings.

The first American figural candy container on record is a glass Liberty Bell that made its debut at the Centennial Exposition in 1876, fittingly held in Philadelphia.

The little bell rang in a new era of novelties. Before the turn of the century, candy-filled guns and railroad lanterns were popular. Vendors on trains or at train stations sold many. Politicians wooing the votes of parents passed out candy to their children in small glass hats. During the 1890s painted and opaque white glass bearing a vacation spot's name in gold script was a favorite with tourists. These souvenirs often took the form of horns, clocks, and suitcases.

Other glass containers commemorated events of historical significance. The invention of the telephone and automobile were hailed in this fashion, as was Lindbergh's Trans-Atlantic flight. Ships, cars, trucks, and airplanes were immortalized in candy-filled glass shapes. So were popular figures, both real and imaginary, from Charlie Chaplin's Little Tramp to Barney Google.

Girls favored household items, like irons and the ever-present baby bottle. Boys begged for guns and lanterns most, but would gladly settle for trains and fire trucks. Birds, whistles, and piggy banks were a hit for both sexes.

Before 1920, candy containers were often hand painted. Production of glass candy containers all but ceased during the Depression, when few families had money to spare on frivolities. By 1940 the glasshouses revved back up. World War II introduced new designs. Jeeps and other military-themed containers were soon to follow, but sugar was in short supply during the war, limiting production.

Plastic changed everything. In the novelty business, it made its presence felt in the late 1940s, first as a minor appendage on glass containers. Plastic soon began to dominate the candy container industry. Kids wanted the bright colors, detail, and moveable parts, and plastic was easier and cheaper to produce in large quantities.

In the 1960s, the move from glass to plastic became complete, except for a limited production of expensive, ornate glass candy containers aimed at adults. New companies started production as the old glass manufacturers and candy-packaging firms went out of business. New York's Selco Novelty Products marketed Candy Mart in 1948 and Allied Molding Corp. of Corona, New York, put out Auto Racer the following year. One of the big early plastic container makers, E. Rosen Co. of Providence, Rhode Island, began turning out its Christmas Bell in 1950. After nearly a half-century of continuous production of candy novelties, family-owned E. Rosen went into receivership and ceased production in 1998.

These products formed the vanguard of plastic candy-containing toys that soon flooded the market. Many had familiar shapes: telephones and dogs, pistols and trains, rabbits and Santa's boots.

Those containers haven't disappeared; they have just been updated year after year, reflecting the times.

A candy container of the 1990s is apt to be a toy cellular phone that beeps at the push of a button. Instead of a locomotive, how about a series of intergalactic space ships?

While Bugs Bunny is as popular as ever, manufacturers now churn out dozens of lines of containers themed after major motion pictures, TV shows, and comic books.

Today, candy novelties are a multibillion-dollar industry, with global distribution by dozens of companies. The products are available just about everywhere, from Toys-R-Us to Wal-Mart, from gas stations to convenience stores.

The sophistication of the current generation of novelties is amazing. These aren't the simple designs of the past, but interactive ones, like wristwatches that pop open to reveal candy balls. Clearly, the line between candy and toy has vanished.

"Products like these are more than just treats," said Larry Graham, president of the National Confectioners Association and Chocolate Manufacturers Association. "The novelty of candy as a toy, as a total experience beyond eating, is an exciting part" of the modern industry.

The experience, however, hasn't changed. Just like in the 1920s, a kid can dig into his pocket for some loose change and buy a candy container. Sweet tooth satisfied, a new toy goes home.

* Glass Candy Containers *

Good reference books on glass candy containers are *The Complete American Glass Candy Containers Handbook*, published by Bowden Publishing; *Collector's Guide to Candy Containers* by Doug Deszo and Rose & Leon Poirer, published by Collector Books; and two books, *An Album of Candy Containers I and II* written and published by Jennie and Thomas Long.

My Thanks to Jennie Long

Jennie Long is a name well known by collectors of glass candy containers.

On December 1, 1999, Jennie Long died at the age of 97. At the age of 67 she started collecting candy containers. In 1978 she wrote her first book, and in 1983 she released her second. Both books have been huge successes, and have always been in demand by collectors and dealers alike. She has received hundreds of letters and phone calls from people seeking her advice and help from all over the U.S., Canada, and England. Jennie has always been happy to share her knowledge with others and has been one of the leading contributors to the hobby of collecting candy containers.

I met Jennie for the first time in 1991. My wife Dolly is a collector of glass candy containers. We met at her home in Kingsburg, California. Her husband had already passed away so we did not have the pleasure of meeting him. We visited about two hours. Jennie was gracious and more than happy to enlighten us about glass candy containers. Her collection was in every room in the house. Displayed in cabinets made by her husband, Tom. My wife was asking Jennie about candy containers, and she was full of good information. One of the things that impressed me personally was when she looked at me and said, "If I were you, I would start collecting plastic candy containers."

I have heard Jennie's voice saying that sentence in my head a hundred times over. I said to myself, take that advice of a person that is older and wiser. I like plastic candy containers, I can afford them, and they are fun to collect, so why not. My wife has her glass candy collection and now I have my plastic collection. Thank you Jennie.

Jack

＊ Today's Interactive Candy Containers ＊

Children's spending power has increased to a staggering $14 billion a year, and children choose candy as the first item they purchase. But today's market has changed. From fast food toys to action figures, pre-teens and adults are demanding a new level of sophistication. And the candy industry is no different. An interactive candy container is a candy-filled toy that you can play with. Not just one that holds candy. Examples would be Ball Catcher, Batman flashlight, Bug City, Candy Crane, Collectable Connectables, etc. Interactive toy candy containers are this generation's choices.

Although the plastic candy container follows a rich tradition of the glass candy containers of the past, this is where the similarity ends. Today's candy containers are more sophisticated; taking advantage of easily manufactured plastic, which provides a countless variety of color and detail. Of more significance is the demand for plastic candy containers has far exceeded that of its predecessor, the glass candy container.

Today's candy container comes in any shape and color that the manufacturer can sell. Most of the containers are imported, mainly from China and Mexico. The candy in them is usually from the United States and Canada.

Some of the many shapes include cars, boats, guns, animals, airplanes, cartoon characters, holiday decorations, mailboxes, hearts, monsters, food items, toys, body parts, telephones, office equipment, bottles, jars, games, bugs, TV & movie characters, cartoon & comic book heroes, etc. You will find just about any popular figure that is hot at the time.

You can find these great little collectibles at grocery stores, toy stores, candy stores, gas stations, convenience stores, department stores, amusement parks, discount stores, flea markets, garage sales, and I have even bought them in a casino in Las Vegas.

They are now showing up in antique and collectible shops and over the Internet.

7

✳ A Note About Values ✳

To give a container an absolute value is unrealistic. The value depends on condition, supply and demand, location, and the desire of the buyer.

1. Condition: Does it have all its parts? Is it scratched? Is it filled with the original candy or gum? Does it have the original label?

2. Supply and demand: If there are a lot available the price may be less. If not, the price will be higher.

3. Location: It seems that the same container will bring a higher price in different parts of the country. But all things do not always hold true for all containers.

4. Bottom line: A container is worth what someone is willing to pay.

The prices that are included in this book are to be used as a guide only. Prices change from day to day, month to month, and year to year. One good thing about that is the direction seems to be *up!*

If you purchase a candy container that you like, and you think you paid a fair price, the enjoyment you will receive for years to come is what makes collecting fun.

✳ Candy Container Companies ✳

Amurol Confection Co.

Amurol was founded in January 1948, by an Illinois dentist, Bruno Petrulis. The first products were ammoniated toothpaste and tooth powder, and the name was routed in the key ingredients: ammonia (AM) and urea (UR). The (OL) comes from "taken orally." It all adds up to Amurol.

Petrulis's quest to promote oral health led him to the other ammonia-laden products, including sugar-free chewing gum. The ammonia in the gum helped counteract acid in the mouth, identified as a major contributor to cavities.

Because Petrulis lacked a chewing gum plant, he merged his company with True Blue Gum Co. in Grand Rapids, Michigan. The company became known as Amurol Products Co. In addition to an assortment of sugar-free gums, the company also produced mints and hard candy.

In 1958, Petrulis sold the company to the William H. Wrigley Jr. Co., the nation's biggest gum maker. About a decade later, Amurol developed the first soft sugar-free bubble gum: Blammo. It was a last nod to Petrulis. In the mid-80s, Amurol dumped the sugar-free line and focused on the novelty gum business.

Today, the Wrigley subsidiary is understandably big on gum, but the recipes are its own. CEO and President A.G. Atwater Jr. is given plenty of independence and for good reason. For the past 20 years, Amurol, based in Yorkville, Illinois, has staked a claim to a large chunk of the highly profitable candy novelty market. Sales in 1997 were estimated at more than $100 million.

Two products have reached near legendary status for their enduring appeal to youngsters. Bubble Tape, introduced in 1988, is the top-selling fruit-flavored bubble gum item in America. It comes in a hinged plastic clamshell that dispenses a six-foot-long roll of gum available in four flavors. Big League Chew, which hit the shelves in 1981, is shredded bubble gum in a foil pouch. It was reportedly inspired by former New York Yankee pitcher Jim Bouton, who was disgusted with the trend of young teenagers emulating major leagues by chewing tobacco.

Taking aim at kids between the ages of 6 and 14, Amurol specializes in low-cost products filled with gum and candy. The company has about 50 items on its price list at any time and the most expensive one retails for $2.99. That's a corporate strategy: Don't expect Amurol to be pushing battery-powered, voice-chip-equipped novelties anytime soon.

"We've been in the novelty business since the mid-70s, and most of what kids want is still under a dollar," said Bruce Thompson, vice president of marketing for Amurol. "It's got to taste good, and it's got to be affordable too. We're not going to compete with Cap Toys."

Other Amurol mainstays include Bug City, Ouch Spots, Squeeze Cone, Cellular Bubble Gum, Game Boy, Bubble Jackpot, and Super Gumputer.

On the licensing front, Amurol has full rights to "Rugrats." The company favors TV shows to movies because of their longer-lasting appeal. One of the company's first licensed novelty products was a Mork Bubble Gum container in 1979.

"All of our successful products have a unique form, a unique, often reusable package, and a theme that ties the package and product together," Thompson said.

The corporate motto may be "Innovation in Kids' Confections," but the key to success is testing the stuff on kids. The Amurol Candy Tasters club features a database of the likes and dislikes of some 3,000 youngsters. Members are frequently called in from the Naperville, Illinois, area to try out the latest offerings and sound off. Out of every 10 items pitched, only one is actually taken to market, Thompson said.

"We get a lot of inspiration from kids. Sometimes we just ask them, 'What's cool? What's happening out there?'"

Berzerk Candy Werks

Berzerk Candy Werks is so irreverent and innovative it's hard to believe it is the spawn of one of the world's biggest corporations.

The mammoth, multibillion-dollar Philip Morris companies include Kraft Food Ingredients (KFI), which in turn created Berzerk in 1991.

Aimed squarely at the hot candy novelties market, Memphis-based Berzerk is a small but nimble operation that prides itself on keeping pace with fast-changing adolescent tastes in toys and candy.

The company got its first products on store shelves six months after starting up, which is nothing short of wondrous. Aggressive marketing is the key to success, according to product manager Angela Stevens. Case in point: Air Gummi, a takeoff on Nike, featuring athletic shoe-shaped gum in a plastic shoebox.

Berzerk signed joint licensing agreements with one of the world's largest toy makers and one of the world's largest media empires, as only a wealthy start-up can do.

The deal with Mattel gave Berzerk access to Hot Wheels and Streex merchandising. One novelty that proved to be a hit was wheel-shaped SweetTarts in a plastic Hot Wheels tire.

Stevens says it's crucial for candy novelty makers to make the products affordable, portable, irreverent, and of relevance to a kid, like sports or toy cars.

"There has to be something slightly fun and slightly irreverent in most of the packaging," she said.

Another hit was Soccer Power Sours, candy shaped like little soccer balls and packed in a small, flat, round container. While Hot Wheels is aimed at boys, ages 3 – 10, soccer is big with older kids of both sexes. The sour candy attracts young teens.

Berzerk also has candy licensing rights to *Mad* magazine, which fits its irreverence and target audience well.

Philip Morris is a $60 billion a year conglomerate, and KFI generates a $1.2 billion slice of that pie.

KFI President Rick Avery offered Berzerk the resources and marketing muscle of a giant company but the autonomy of a small start-up. Berzerk organized its own distribution network, using tobacco and candy wholesalers, and also developed free-standing floor displays.

Interactive novelties produced by the company include Candy Pager, a battery-operated toy that beeps and gives electronic messages like "Later, Dude" and "Get Real." It's filled with Tropical Smarties. Another battery-powered item, Candy Keyboard, is filled with Smarties. It can play a half-dozen songs and comes with a songbook.

This candy container is what is known as a presentation container. Hershey Chocolate U.S.A., a division of Hershey Foods, used the one pictured. The container was filled with a new product, in this case, "Classic Caramels." This was their introduction to the chewy candy category. A salesperson would use this container at a headquarter presentation to gain acceptance of the item and an authorization to distribute it to all stores. The salesperson contacted a buyer and presented this to him in the hopes of obtaining a purchase order for the candy. The container is not for sale to the general public, and to obtain one is very rare. This one was given to me by Thomas J. Kennedy, Sacramento district manager of the San Francisco region.

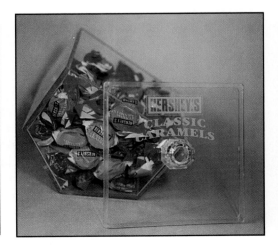

Cap Toys

Cap Toys was founded by John Osher, the son of a prominent Cincinnati neurosurgeon. Osher started the company in 1987, lost big on some initial toys, but rebounded with a string of hits, including Arcade Basketball.

The Bedford Heights, Ohio, company started manufacturing candy novelties in the early 1990s and quickly established itself as a leader in the field. The company also offers a full line of toys and children's sporting goods. Annual sales are over $100 million, with 118 employees on the payroll. Cap Toys now puts $50 million a year in what it calls interactive candy sales. The company also has licensing rights to Batman and Star Wars.

Toy giant Hasbro, of Pawtucket, Rhode Island, acquired Cap Toys in 1997. In hopes of capturing bigger profits in candy novelties, the parent company launched its Hasbro candy line the same year, based on some of its bestselling games and toys. Offerings included a Mr. Potato Head filled with tart candy and Barrel of Monkeys with gummy candy.

Cap Toys is now a division of OddzOn Inc.

The full array of OddzOn Inc. products are sold through a diverse network of retail outlets — mass market, specialty toy, gift, sporting goods, drug stores, video stores, bookstores, supermarkets, and department stores nationwide. Selected products are sold in over 50 countries.

Ce De Candy

This company is best known for producing Smarties, the little rolls of candy tablets that have become a Halloween staple. New Jersey-based Ce De Candy Inc. is also a successful maker of candy novelties.

The company's candy necklaces on stretch strings have recently enjoyed a faddish rebirth, with pop stars and supermodels like Cindy Crawford seen sporting them.

In 1949, founder and chairman of the board Edward Dee immigrated to America from Great Britain, where he had a background in the candy business.

Dee decided to start out by imitating a proven winner in Europe: pressed-dextrose candy tablets. While Nestlé owned the trade name Smarties in other countries for a chocolate candy similar to M & M's, Dee was able to get rights to the name in America.

Smarties have always been a big seller, and continue to be the company's mainstay. Annual sales of all products are estimated at $10 million.

The Dee family still owns the company, with manufacturing plants in Union, New Jersey; Newmarket, Ontario; and North Charleston; South Carolina. Jonathan Dee is the company president.

Ce De Candy launched its novelty line in 1957. Products include Candy Rings, Candy Lipstick, Candy Watches, Candy Money, and Candy-filled Fruits, the latter a series of fruit-shaped containers filled with powder candy.

One of the more imaginative offerings was the CD 2000 space fleet: candy-filled spaceships that "dock" with one another.

Creative Confection Concepts

Creative Confection hasn't grabbed a lot of attention in the mainstream media with dazzling interactive novelties, but it has nonetheless quietly gained in popularity.

The Milwaukee-based company has a long line of novelties that have proven popular with kids. Starting in 1995, the company established itself in foreign markets.

In the U.S., Creative Confections has gained exclusive rights to manufacture and sell novelties based on feature films, including *Ace Ventura*, *Space Jam*, and *Batman and Robin*. More importantly, the company makes and distributes Warner Brothers products, including Looney Tunes characters.

Creative Confections also does its own thing, putting flavored bubble gum in plastic containers shaped like fruits and vegetables, human body parts (Bubble Thumb is one), dinosaurs, golf clubs — even the patriotic Bubble Flag.

Blo Banana and the pickle-shaped Piccolo double as whistles when the candy's gone. "Gum and Toy in One!" exclaims the promotional materials.

Biker Buddies, a set of four brightly-colored grimacing "crazy dudes," are designed to hang on a child's bicycle handlebars.

"We would like to be known for our unique plastic container toys that appeal to every young child with a sweet tooth," said Douglas Bartelt, public relations director.

The Topps Company

In 1938, four Brothers, Abraham, Ira, Philip, and Joseph Shorin, founded Topps Chewing Gum in Brooklyn, New York.

The company went on to become the world's best-known manufacturer of bubble gum and trading cards, with products sold in 40 countries.

Their original concept was to market a product with consumer appeal that could carry a brand name and be consumable. They began by marketing single pieces of conventional chewing gum, priced at a penny a piece.

The company name, Topps, evolved from the Shorins' goal of making it "tops" in the field, with the extra "p" added for distinctive identity. During World War II, the company's defense-minded slogan, "Don't Talk Chum, Chew Topps Gum," became a catchphrase for soldiers and civilians working in defense plants. After the war, Topps developed its famous Bazooka bubble gum, originally sold for a nickel. In 1953, the Bazooka Joe character was introduced — a kid with a baseball cap and eye patch (added by the creative department for distinctiveness).

From time to time the company has created products parodying popular fads and recognized products. These products have included Nasty Valentines, Wacky Packages, and gum and candy containers molded to the shape of popular TV and movie characters. A group led by Forstmann Little & Co. and Topps management in 1984 acquired Topps in a leveraged buyout acquisition.

The company moved into new headquarters at the Topps building in lower Manhattan in 1994.

* Candy Containers *

Airplane

Category: Transportation
Contents: Colored candy balls
Size: 1¾"h, 4³⁄₁₆"w, 4½"d
Made for: Allen Mitchell Products, Oxnard, CA 93030
Made in: Hong Kong
Cost new: $0.59/**Value:** $5.00 – 7.00
Description: Biplane, four wheels, three-blade prop.

Airplane (bi-plane bank)

Category: Transportation
Contents: Colored gumballs, 3 oz.
Size: 3³⁄₁₆"h, 5⁵⁄₁₆"w, 5⁹⁄₁₆"d
Made for: Bee International, Chula Vista, CA 91912
Made in: China
Cost new: $2.99/**Value:** $4.00 – 5.00
Description: Has paper sticker of a pilot, head only, with an old cap and goggles. Has coin slot for use as a bank. Three wheels and propeller are moveable. Embossed on bottom of the left wing: "Made in China."

Airplane (double tail)

Category: Transportation
Contents: Small colored balls
Size: ⁷⁄₁₆"h, 3"w, 2⅞"d
Made in: West Germany
Value: $4.00 – 5.00
Description: Has a paper closure underneath and "W. Germany" embossed beneath the right wing.

Aladdin's Lamp

Category: Miscellaneous
Contents: Small colored candy balls, 0.5 oz.
Size: 1¹⁵⁄₁₆"h, 1⅝"w, 3⅝"d
Made for: Novelty Opecialtieb Inc., Campbell, CA
Made in: Taiwan
Cost new: $0.65/**Value:** $3.00 – 4.50
Description: Closure is plastic and screw-on. Purchased in 1995 at Marine World in Vallejo, California.

Alligator

Category: Animals
Contents: Colored candy, 0.31 oz.
Size: 1"h, 1⁹⁄₁₆"w, 3¾"d
Made for: Phila Chewing Gum Corp., Havertown, PA 19038
Made in: U.S.A.
Cost new: $0.69/**Value:** $4.00 – 6.00

Description: Embossed on the under side of the mouth is "Net Wt. .31 oz 8.8g." Embossed on the bottom: "candy: dextrose, citric acid, magnesium stearate, art. flavors, colors (FD & C yellow no. 5), phila. chewing gum corp. Havertown PA 19038. made in U.S.A." The candy is in the shape of a knife, watch, shoe, and hand.

Alf

Category: Characters
Contents: Pellet candy shaped like cats
Size: 2½"h, 1⁹⁄₁₆"w, 1⅜"d
Made for: Alien Prod.
Made in: China
Value: $8.00 – 10.00
Description: Has "© 1987 ALIEN PROD." embossed on the bottom.

Alien

Category: Bottles and jars
Contents: Powder candy
Size: 3½"h, 1⁷⁄₁₆"w
Cost new: $0.35/**Value:** $3.00 – 4.00
Description: I purchased this container in Yuma, Arizona, 1996. It has no label or markings. It looks like a water bottle with a bug's head on it. The tongue is sticking out of a smiling face. I think this came from Mexico.

Alien (candy machine)

Category: Characters
Contents: Fruit flavored candy balls, 1 oz.
Size: 5½"h, 2¼"w, 2½"d
Made for: Candy Containers and More, Oxnard, CA 93030
Made in: China
Cost new: $0.99/**Value:** $2.50 – 4.00
Description: Embossed on the bottom: "© 1997 Sunco – Patent Pending – P NO. 7468820 – MADE IN CHINA. To refill, Remove head by turning counterclockwise. To dispense candy: Place on level surface, turn handle left or right. Item no. 9040."

Apolo

Category: Miscellaneous
Contents: Glucose liquid, 24g
Size: 5⅞"h, 1⅝"w, 1⅛"d
Made for: Lorena Products Inc., Zapoan, Jalisco, Mexico
Made in: Mexico
Cost new: $0.35/**Value:** $3.00 – 4.00
Description: Paper label reads: "APOLO – UF-14" and has picture of a space man holding up two fingers. Resembles hypodermic.

Apothecary Jar (rabbit)

Category: Bottles and jars
Contents: Jelly beans, 4 oz.
Size: 5¹³⁄₁₆"h, 2³⁄₁₆"w
Made for: Ameri-suisse, Elizabeth, NJ 07201
Made in: U.S.A.
Cost new: $2.24/**Value:** $3.00 – 4.00
Description: Embossed under the paper label on the bottom: "4 oz. JAR S&L Plastics, Inc. Nazareth, PA." The jar is clear plastic and the rabbit stands on top.

Apothecary Jar (rabbit, paper under arm)

Category: Bottles and jars
Contents: Jelly beans, 4 oz.
Size: 6⅛"h, 2³⁄₁₆"w
Made for: Ameri-suisse, Elizabeth, NJ 07201
Made in: U.S.A.
Cost new: $2.24/**Value:** $3.00 – 4.00
Description: Embossed under the paper label on the bottom: "4 oz. JAR S&L Plastics, Inc. Nazareth, PA." The jar is clear plastic and the rabbit stands on top.

Apple

Category: Food items
Contents: Candy, ⅝ oz.
Size: 2⁹⁄₁₆"h, 1⅝"w, 1⅜"d
Made for : Ce De Candy, Inc. Union, NJ 07083
Made in: U.S.A.
Cost new: $0.40/**Value:** $1.50 – 2.00
Description: Filled with powder candy. Comes with a paper label under the screw cap. Cap has a ring for a string. Can be used as an ornament.

Apple (Taffy)

Category: Food items
Contents: Gum, 1.7 oz.
Size: 2⅜"h, 3⅛"w, 2¼"d
Made for: Creative Confection Concepts, Milwaukee, WI 53209
Made in: Mexico
Cost new: $1.19/**Value:** $4.00 – 6.50
Description: Label between apple and worm reads: "Taffy Apple." Worm is the closure. Caramel flavor on the outside. Apple flavor inside. Bought new in 1997.

Babs Bunny

Category: Animals
Contents: Sugarless candy, 0.2 oz
Size: 3¼"h, 2¼"w, 1½"d
Made for: Topps Co., Duryea, PA 18642
Made in: China
Cost new: $0.99/**Value:** $4.00 – 6.00
Description: Head only. Top label reads: "Tiny Toon Adventures." Bottom label: "™ & © 1991 Warner Bros. Inc."

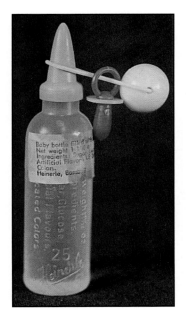

Baby Bottle (Heinerle)

Category: Bottles and jars
Contents: Candy, 1¹⁄₁₀ oz.
Size: 4⁷⁄₁₆"h, 1¹⁄₁₆"w
Made for: Heinerle, Bamberg, Germany
Made in: Germany
Value: $14.00 – 18.00
Description: Baby bottle comes with a rattle and pacifier. Label is in English on plain paper. Embossed on the bottom: "Made in Germ." Embossed on front: "25 Heinerle."

Baby Bottle (Hugo Hein)

Category: Bottles and jars
Contents: Candy, 50g
Size: 4¹⁄₁₆"h, 1¼"w
Made for: Hugo Hein, Bamberg, Germany
Made in: West Germany
Value: $9.00 – 12.00
Description: Label reads: "50g Hugo Hein KG 86 Bamberg. LIEBES PERLEN mit Farbstoff." Has boy holding the name "Heinerle." This container has the remnant of a nipple, which has rotted away. One side of the bottle is marked "50, 100, 150, and 200." Embossed: "Hugo Hein KG," picture of boy, "Bamberg," and "50."

Baby Bottle (with toy)

Category: Bottles and jars
Contents: Gum
Size: 3⅞"h, 1⅛"w
Cost new: $0.50 \ **Value:** $2.00 – 3.00
Description: Has nipple pointed down and nipple cover as closure. Embossed on the sides are volume measurements. One side oz., the other cc. Has toy inside with gum.

Baby Lucas (shaker)

Category: Miscellaneous
Contents: Candy, 0.71 oz.
Size: 1⅞"h, 1¼"w
Made for: Alimentos Matre
Made in: Mexico
Cost new: $0.50 \ **Value:** $1.00 – 2.00
Description: Looks like a salt shaker. Has powder candy inside. Paper label reads: "Baby Lucas sweet & sour candy powder polvo acidulce."

Bagheera (Disney's Jungle Book)

Category: Animals
Contents: Nerds
Size: 3"h, 1⅞"w, 3¹¹⁄₁₆"d
Made for: McDonalds Corp., Oak Brook, IL
Made in: China
Cost new: free w/Happy Meal \ **Value:** $1.00 – 2.00
Description: Marketed as McDonald's Happy Meal toy. One of a series from the Disney animated movie. Plastic wrap it came in has messages in English, French, and Spanish. Candy came in a separate package.

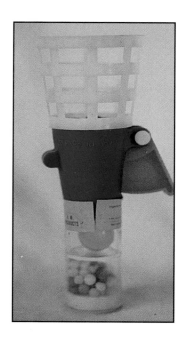

Ball Catcher

Category: Games
Contents: Small colored candy balls, 0.12 oz.
Size: 4⅝"h, 2¼"w, 1¾"d
Made for: Allen Mitchell Products, U.S.A.
Made in: Hong Kong
Cost new: $0.65 \ **Value:** $5.50 – 7.50
Description: Comes with ball in the middle, candy at bottom. To play the game you catch the ball in the basket, squeeze trigger, launching ball in the air.

Banana

Category: Food items
Contents: Powdered candy, ⅝ oz.
Size: 3¹⁵⁄₁₆"h, 1⅛"w
Made for: Ce De Candy Inc., Union, NJ 07083
Made in: U.S.A.
Cost new: $1.19 \ **Value:** $1.25 – 2.00
Description: Paper a label under the screw cap. Cap has a ring for hanging as an ornament.

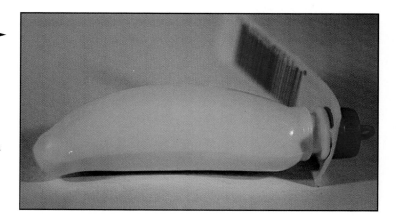

Banana (Go Bananas!)

Category: Food items
Contents: Gum, 1.7 oz.
Size: 6½"h, 1½"w, 1⅝"d
Made for: Creative Confection Concepts, Milwaukee, WI 53209
Made in: Mexico
Cost new: $1.19 \ **Value:** $5.00 – 7.00
Description: Has a plastic cord attached, can be worn around the neck. Label reads: "Banana cream flavored bubble gum. GO BANANAS!" © 1997.

Banana (whistle)

Category: Food items
Contents: Gum, 0.5 oz.
Size: 4"h, 1"w, 1⅛"d
Made for: Creative Confection Concepts, Milwaukee, WI 53209
Made in: China
Cost new: $1.19 \ **Value:** $5.00 – 7.00
Description: Gum and toy in one. Banana cream bubble gum inside banana-shaped whistle. Has a plastic cord to be worn around the neck. Embossed on the back: "Made in Mexico, CCC, LLC."

Bank (Candy Mart)

Category: Gumball Dispensers
Contents: Gum
Size: 5¼"h, 3¼"w, 2⅛"d
Made for: Selco Novelty Products Inc., L.I. City, NY
Made in: U.S.A.
Value: $35.00 – 50.00
Description: Comes in a box that reads: "Candy Mart Bank — A Real Vending Machine." Embossed on the back "Patents Pending — Selco Novelty Products Inc. — L.I. City, N.Y. — Made in U.S.A." There is a coin slot on the side and a door on the back to remove coins. It comes in red, yellow, and green.

Barbie (tin box)

Category: Nonplastic
Contents: Chocolates, ⅞ oz.
Size: 1"h, 4⅜"w, 3¾"d
Made for: Russell Stover Candies, Kansas City, MO 64106
Made in: China
Value: $1.50 – 2.00
Description: Bottom of tin container reads: "BARBIE Chocolates – Collect All Eight Surprise Stamps."

Barbie (egg)

Category: Nonplastic
Contents: Chocolates, 3 oz.
Size: 2¾"h, 2½"w, 4⅜"d
Made for: Russell Stover Candies, Kansas City, MO 64106
Made in: China
Cost new: $2.57 Wal-Mart \ **Value:** $2.50 – 3.50
Description: Egg is made of tin. Made in 1996.

Barbie (heart)

Category: Nonplastic
Contents: Solid milk chocolate hearts
Size: 4½"h, 4⅞"w, 1¼"d
Made for: Russell Stover Candies, Kansas City, MO 64106
Made in: China
Cost new: $3.59 \ **Value:** $3.50 – 4.50
Description: © 1997 Mattel, Inc. Heart shaped tin container, filled with solid milk chocolate hearts. Barbie is a trademark owned and used under license from Mattel, Inc. All rights reserved.

Barfo (dad)

Category: Characters
Contents: Liquid candy, 0.5 oz.
Size: 3"h, 1⅛"w
Made for: The Topps Co., Duryea, PA 18642
Made in: Hong Kong
Value: $6.00 – 7.50
Description: Made like a bellows. You would push to get the liquid candy out. Comes with a stopper in their mouth. Has purple liquid candy in it. © 1989.

Barfo (dog)

Category: Characters
Contents: Liquid candy, 0.5 oz.
Size: 2¾"h, 1⅛"w
Made for: The Topps Co., Duryea, PA 18642
Made in: Hong Kong
Value: $6.00 – 7.50
Description: Made like a bellows. You would push to get the liquid candy out. Comes with a stopper in their mouth. Has red liquid candy in it. © 1989.

Barfo (Jr.)

Category: Characters
Contents: Liquid candy, 0.5 oz.
Size: 3"h, 1⅛"w
Made for: The Topps Co., Duryea, PA 18642
Made in: Hong Kong
Value: $6.00 – 7.50
Description: Made like a bellows. You would push to get the liquid candy out. Comes with a stopper in their mouth. Has red liquid candy in it. © 1989.

Barfo (mom)

Category: Characters
Contents: Liquid candy, 0.5 oz.
Size: 3"h, 1⅛"w
Made for: The Topps Co., Duryea, PA 18642
Made in: Hong Kong
Value: $6.00 – 7.50
Description: Made like a bellows. You would push to get the liquid candy out. Comes with a stopper in their mouth. Has red liquid candy in it. © 1989.

Barrel of Monkeys

Category: Miscellaneous
Contents: Chewy candy
Size: 3½"h, 2¼"w
Made for: Hasbro Inc., Pawtucket, RI 02862
Made in: Mexico
Cost new: $2.99 Las Vegas \ **Value:** $4.50 – 6.00
Description: Covered with clear plastic wrap. Paper label on the bottom reads: "Barrel of Candy Monkeys. P/N47583601." They come in different colors and flavors. This one is cherry flavor. Has a monkey and the words "Barrel of Monkeys" embossed on the top of container. It looks like the game only smaller.

Baseball (gum machine)

Category: Gumball dispensers
Contents: Gum, 2.0 oz.
Size: 3¾"h, 2¼"w
Made for: Bee International, Chula Vista, CA 91912
Made in: China
Cost new: $0.99 \ **Value:** $3.00 – 4.00
Description: Embossed on the bottom: "© 1997 C. L. MADE IN CHINA." Embossed on the front are three bees. Turn the handle and the gum comes out. It is also made with a basketball, football, and soccerball.

Baseball (gumball machine)

Category: Gumball dispensers
Contents: Gumballs, 1.1 oz.
Size: 4"h, 2⅜"w, 2¾"d
Made for: Candy Containers & More Inc., Oxnard, CA 93030
Made in: China
Cost new: $0.95 \ **Value:** $3.00 – 4.00
Description: Comes in different colors. Turn handle on the front to get gumballs. Under paper label is embossed: "PATENT PENDING MADE IN CHINA."

Baseball (with hat)

Category: Miscellaneous
Contents: Gum, 1.5 oz.
Size: 3³⁄₁₆"h, 3¹⁄₈"w, 3⅜"d
Made for: Hilco Corporation, Norristown, PA 19401
Made in: China
Cost new: $0.97 Wal-Mart \ **Value:** $4.00 – 5.00
Description: Embossed on the bottom: "© 1994 Hilco China."
The cap has a hole in the back, twist cap to dispense gumballs.

Baseball Bat

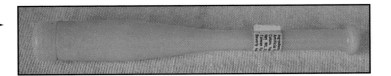

Category: Miscellaneous
Contents: Powered candy, 0.14 oz.
Size: 4⁵⁄₁₆"h, ½"w
Made for: Bee International, Beverly Hills, CA 90058
Made in: Taiwan
Value: $6.50 – 8.00
Description: Made of soft plastic with a screw-on closure on the end. Notice the address of Bee International. There are no markings on this container.

Baseball Bat (Pro Ball)

Category: Miscellaneous
Contents: Bubble gum balls, 6.6 oz.
Size: 17⅞"h, 1¾"w
Made for: Concord Confections Inc., Concord, Ontario, Canada L4K 3N1
Made in: Canada
Cost new: $3.00 \ **Value:** $4.00 – 6.00
Description: Embossed on the clear part of the bat is "Concord Confections Inc., Concord, Ont., Canada." It came with two paper labels. One glued on the bat and one made of cardboard wrapped around the bat. Label reads "For kids of all ages! Pro ball Bubble Gum Bat. net wt. 6.6 oz."

Baseball Player #361501

Category: Characters
Contents: Colored candy, 1¼ oz.
Size: 4½"h, 1¾"w, 1⁷⁄₁₆"d
Made for: E. Rosen Company, Pawtucket, RI 02860
Made in: Hong Kong
Value: $7.00 – 9.00
Description: Boy has a ball, glove, and baseball cap. The body is clear and the head is the closure and is painted. Label on the bottom "#361501."

Basket (bunny in egg)

Category: Holiday
Contents: Jelly beans
Size: 3⅜"h, 3³⁄₁₆"w, 2⅜"d
Made for: Hilco Corp., Norristown, PA 19401
Made in: China
Cost new: $0.59 \ **Value:** $2.00 – 4.00
Description: Bunny on his back in half eggshell, with hands and feet out. There is a string through left ear for use as an ornament. Basket textured to resemble wood. Slates on four sides. © 1998.

Basket (See's)

Category: Holiday
Contents: See's candy
Size: 3⁵⁄₁₆"h, 3⅛"w, 2⅜"d
Made for: See's Candy Shops Inc., Los Angeles, CA
Made in: China
Value: $2.50 – 3.50
Description: Basket is solid on ends, with slats front and back. Illustrated wreath has red bow on top and "See's" in center; red, blue, and yellow dots.

Basketball (gum machine)

Category: Gumball dispensers
Contents: Gum, 2.0 oz.
Size: 3¾"h, 2¼"w
Made for: Bee International, Chula Vista, CA 91912
Made in: China
Cost new: $0.99 \ **Value:** $2.00 – 3.00
Description: Embossed on the bottom: "© 1997 C. L. MADE IN CHINA." Embossed on the front are three bees. Turn the handle and the gum comes out. It is also made with a football, baseball, and soccerball.

Basketball (gumball machine)

Category: Gumball dispensers
Contents: Gumballs, 1.1 oz.
Size: 4"h, 2⅜"w, 2¹¹⁄₁₆"d
Made for: Candy Containers & More Inc., Oxnard, CA 93030
Made in: China
Cost new: $0.95 \ **Value:** $2.00 – 3.00
Description: Comes in different colors. Turn handle on the front to get gumballs. Under paper label is embossed: "PATENT PENDING MADE IN CHINA."

Batman

Category: Characters
Contents: Gum, 2.3 oz.
Size: 4⁹⁄₁₆"h, 2⁹⁄₁₆"w, 2¾"d
Made for: Creative Confection Concepts, Milwaukee, WI 53209
Made in: Mexico
Cost new: $2.29 \ **Value:** $4.50 – 8.00
Description: Head only. Container is flat in back, with a picture of Batgirl on it. © 1997, DC Comics.

Batman (1989)

Category: Characters
Contents: Pill-shaped candy, 0.2 oz.
Size: 2⁷⁄₁₆"h, 1¹¹⁄₁₆"w, 1"d
Made for: The Topps Co., Duryea, PA 18642
Made in: Hong Kong
Value: $6.00 – 7.50
Description: © DC Comics Inc. 1989. The candy has a bat on one side and the word "Batman" on the other.

Batman (bust)

Category: Characters
Contents: Gum, 0.4 oz.
Size: 2⅝"h, 2⁵⁄₁₆"w, 1⅜"d
Made for: Topps Co., Duryea, PA 18642
Made in: China
Cost new: $0.97 \ **Value:** $3.00 – 4.50
Description: Head and shoulders of Batman. White eyes, flesh-colored face. Embossed on the back: "DC COMICS 1995."

Batman (flashlight)

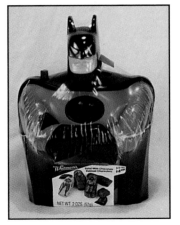

Category: Characters
Contents: Milk chocolate, 2 oz.
Size: 6"h, 4¼"w, 3¼"d
Made for: Whitman's Candies, Kansas City, MO 64106
Made in: China
Cost new: $4.95 \ **Value:** $6.00 – 8.00
Description: Has belt hook on back, embossed with "Whitman's™ & © 1997 DC Comics." On front is label that reads "Whitman's Solid Milk Chocolate Batman Characters." Candy is shaped like Batman, Robin, and The Joker. Has a button on Batman's right shoulder that operates flashlight.

Batman (head)

Category: Characters
Contents: Candy, 0.4oz.
Size: 2⅝"h, 1¼"w (at base), 1½"d
Made for: Topps Co., Duryea, PA 18642
Made in: China\Hong Kong
Cost new: $0.59 \ **Value:** $5.00 – 10.00
Description: Eyes are white, face is flesh colored. Embossed on bottom: "1989 DC COMICS INC." Comes in black and in blue. Black was made in Hong Kong.

Bear (Candy Pet)

Category: Animals
Contents: Colored candy beads
Size: 2⅞"h, 1⅞"w, 1⅝"d
Made for: Wizard Toys Inc., Bell, CA 90201
Made in: China
Value: $3.00 – 4.00
Description: There are six different Wizard Candy Pets: Bear, Cat, Chick, Dog, Duck, and Pig. They are sold on a card. Net Wt. 1 oz. The hat is the closure. Candy made in Canada. Item 7100.

Bear (See's)

Category: Nonplastic
Contents: Chocolate candy, 2 oz.
Size: 4¾"h, 2⁵⁄₁₆"w, 1⅜"d
Made for: See's Candy Shops, Inc., Los Angeles, CA
Made in: China
Value: $2.00 – 2.50
Description: Made of tin. Has a gold cord at the top to be used as a Christmas ornament. Bear has a Santa's hat on and is holding candy canes and a present.

Bear Bank

Category: Animals
Contents: Candy, 2.25 oz.
Size: 5¾"h, 6⁵⁄₁₆"w, 1¹³⁄₁₆"d
Made for: Candy Containers & More Inc., Oxnard, CA 93030
Made in: China
Cost new: $1.99 \ **Value:** $3.00 – 4.00
Description: Paper label on the bottom of the container. Clear plastic window shows candy inside container. Has a coin slot on top with a sticker covering the slot. Front and back are made the same.

Bed Bugs

Category: Miscellaneous
Contents: Pressed candy in shape of bugs, 0.35oz.
Size: 1½"h, 1½"w, 2¾"d
Made for: Fleer Corp., Phila., PA 19141
Value: $4.50 – 6.50
Description: Comes in blue, orange, red, and yellow. Embossed on the bottom: "Bed Bugs™ CANDY – (has ingredients) – © Fleer Corp. Phila. Pa 19141 NET WT. .35 OZ."

Bedrock Boulder

Category: Miscellaneous
Contents: Soft-centered rock candy, 2 oz.
Size: 1⅞"h, 2½"w, 3½"d
Made for: Creative Confection Concepts Inc.
Value: $3.00 – 5.00
Description: Produced following release of "The Flintstones" movie. Made in 1993.

Beeper Candy (X-Men)

Category: Battery operated
Contents: Gum, 1.5 oz.
Size: 3⁹⁄₁₆"h, 2⅞"w, 1¼"d
Made for: Classic Heroes Inc., Stuart, FL 34995
Made in: China
Value: $2.50 – 4.00
Description: Top paper label reads "1-800-X-Men." Front label: "Marvel Comics, X-MEN, electronic Beeper Candy." Belt clip on the back. Made in 1995.

Bell (with candy)

Category: Miscellaneous
Contents: Individually wrapped in red foil, 4 oz.
Size: 7"h, 4³⁄₁₆"w
Made for: Kmart Corp., Troy, MI 48084
Made in: China
Cost new: $2.99 \ **Value:** $4.00 – 5.50
Description: Comes with a gold and red ribbon, sleigh bell and card to put name of the person receiving and sending bell.

Big Baby

Category: Bottles and jars
Contents: Colored candy stars, 1.4 oz.
Size: 4⁵⁄₁₆"h, 1½"w
Made for: Albert & Son Inc., Greenwich, CT 06830
Made in: China
Cost new: $1.19 \ **Value:** $2.00 – 3.00
Description: Baby bottle with rubber nipple. Embossed on the back are measurements: "10 – 20 – 30 – 40 – 50 – and 60." Front of the label reads "Will you be my BIG BABY?" Container also comes in clear bag with cardboard label attached to bag.

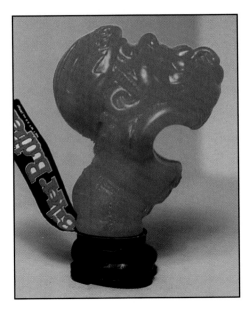

Biker Buddy (Crash Test)

Category: Characters
Contents: Gum, 3 oz.
Size: 4⅞"h, 2⁷⁄₁₆"w, 3³⁄₁₆"d
Made for: Creative Confection Concepts, Milwaukee, WI 53209
Made in: Mexico
Cost new: $2.29 \ **Value:** $4.50 – 6.00
Description: Made to fit on bicycle handlebar. Has "Crash Test" on helmet, "Biker Buddies" on belly. Tongue hangs out, eyes are crossed. Series of four: Crash Test, Basket Case, Road Rash, and Skid Kid.

Birdie (McDonald's)

Category: Characters
Contents: Nerds
Size: 2⁹⁄₁₆"h, 1⅞"w, 1⁷⁄₁₆"d
Made for: McDonalds Corp., Oak Brook, IL 60521
Made in: China
Cost new: free w/Happy Meal \ **Value:** $1.00 – 2.00
Description: Marketed as McDonald's Happy Meal toy. One of a series of six. This is #2. Plastic wrap has messages in English, French, and Spanish. It comes with a separate bag of Wonka Spooky Nerds candy. You can lift the mask on the container to see the character and put the candy in. The mask is the closure. Also there is a spring-loaded door on the bottom. Embossed on the bottom of the container is "© 1998 McDonald's Corp. China HF Chine."

Blender

Category: Miscellaneous
Contents: Gum
Size: 3⅝"h, 1⅞"w, 2¹⁄₁₆"d
Made in: Mexico
Cost new: $0.50 \ **Value:** $3.00 – 4.00
Description: This container has a cord coming from the rear, with a plastic end to resemble an electric plug. It has a paper label that reads "Licua Made in Mexico 2001." The closure is the top of the blender.

Blimpy

Category: Characters
Contents: Jelly beans
Size: 11¾"h, 1¾"w, 2¹⁄₁₆"d
Made for: Bee International, Chula Vista, CA 91912
Value: $1.00 – 2.00
Description: This is sometimes called a candy tube.

Boat (paddle wheeler)

Category: Transportation
Contents: Candy beads
Size: 2¹¹⁄₁₆"h, 1⅛"w, 4½"d
Made for: Allen Mitchell Products, Oxnard, CA 93030
Made in: Hong Kong
Cost new: $0.59 \ **Value:** $4.50 – 6.50
Description: Paddle wheeler has three decks, four smokestacks. Eight windows on top deck, 14 on middle and lower decks.

Boba Fett (Star Wars)

Category: Characters
Contents: Colored pellets, 0.7 oz.
Size: 2⁷⁄₁₆"h, 1⅝"w, 1⅝"d
Made for: Topps Co., Duryea, PA 18642
Made in: Hong Kong
Value: $4.50 – 7.00
Description: From the Stars Wars sequel. Embossed on closure: "Star Wars The Empire Strikes Back." Embossed on back of the head: "© 1980 LFL." To get candy out, turn closure to hole in container.

Bodys

Category: Miscellaneous
Contents: Candy, 0.42 oz.
Size: 3"h, 1"w, 1⁵⁄₁₆"d
Made for: Pez-Haas Inc., Orange, CT 06477
Made in: Spain
Value: $2.50 – 3.50
Description: Bag of candy inside. Hat is the closure.

BomVas

Category: Miscellaneous
Contents: Spicy candy and gum, 1.3 oz.
Size: 2⅛"h, 1¾"w
Made for: Alimentos Matre S.A. DE C.V., Sta. Catarina, Mexico
Made in: Mexico
Cost new: $0.59 \ **Value:** $2.00 – 3.00
Description: Closure is a push-on. Has spoon attached to be removed and used. Paper label reads "Lucas – BomVas – Hot and spicy candy with a BUBBLE GUM." Embossed on the spoon and closure is picture of a duck. Embossed on the bottom: "Pat. Pend. BYESA." Comes in other colors.

Bottle (Bellows Lucas)

Category: Bottles and jars
Contents: Liquid candy, 1.3 oz
Size: 3⅛"h, 1½"w
Made for: Alimentos Matre S.A. DE C.V., Sta. Catarina, Mexico
Made in: Mexico
Cost new: $0.45 \ **Value:** $2.00 – 3.00
Description: Paper label reads "Tamarind Candy LUCAS Dulce De Tamarindo gusano®."

Bottle (PeñaPiel)

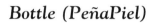

Category: Bottles and jars
Contents: Small colored balls
Size: 1⅞"h, ¾"w
Cost new: $0.10 \ **Value:** $2.00 – 3.00
Description: This container was purchased in Yuma, Arizona, in 1998. The label reads "AGUA NATURAL PEÑAPIEL DE MANANTIAL NO RETORNABLE CONTENIDO NETO 600 LTS." It has no other markings. I would guess this came from Mexico.

Bottle (water whistle)

Category: Bottles and jars
Contents: Gum
Size: 2¹⁵⁄₁₆"h, 1⅛"w
Cost new: $0.35 \ **Value:** $3.00 – 4.50
Description: This container was purchased in Yuma, Arizona, in 1998. The label reads "AGUA CLARA," and has a picture of a book sitting on the beach drinking out of a glass with a straw. There is a beach ball, picnic basket, and blanket next to him. It has no other markings. I would guess this came from Mexico. It is shaped like a 5 gal. water bottle with a whistle on top.

Bottle (whistle)

Category: Bottles and jars
Contents: Gum
Size: 4⅜"h, 1"w
Cost new: $0.25 \ **Value:** $3.00 – 4.00
Description: Closure is a whistle. Purchased in Yuma, Arizona, in 1997. Has paper a label with the word "RAGO" on it. Also in small print: "contenido neto: 500ml." Probably made in Mexico.

Bottles (cola)

Category: Bottles and jars
Contents: Small round balls
Size: 2¹⁵⁄₁₆"h, ¾"w
Cost new: $0.30 \ **Value:** $2.00 – 3.00
Description: The bottles are made a little different from one another but not much. The red bottle's label reads: "barrillitos," and the black bottle's label reads: "Mexi-Cola." The cap presses on. I purchased these in Yuma, and guess they came from Mexico.

Braids (Pooh)

Category: Miscellaneous
Contents: Small candy beads
Size: Braid ¾"h, 1¾"w, ¼"d; Candy tube 12¼"l, ³⁄₁₆" outer diameter
Made for: Tapper Candy Inc., Cleveland, OH 44146
Made in: China
Cost new: $0.99 \ **Value:** $2.50 – $3.50
Description: It was sold as a party favor. Comes four on a card. No. 12007 Candy Net Wt. .37 oz © Disney.

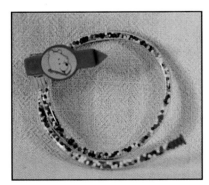

Bubble Beeper

Category: Miscellaneous
Contents: Gum
Size: 3³⁄₁₆"h, 1⅞"w, 1½"d
Made for: Amurol Products Co., Naperville, IL 60566
Made in: U.S.A.
Cost new: $1.19 \ **Value:** $2.00 – 3.00
Description: Contains 17 sticks of bubble gum. Embossed on top right side: "PUSH HERE." Embossed on the bottom: "Amurol Products Company - Patent Pending made in U.S.A."

Bubble Brain

Category: Miscellaneous
Contents: Gum, 2.5 oz.
Size: 2⅛"h, 3¼"w, 3⅞"d
Made for: Creative Confection Concepts Inc., Milwaukee, WI 53209
Made in: Mexico
Value: $4.00 – 6.00
Description: Wrapped with plastic that reads "Bubble Brain bubble gum. 5 free brain twisters trivia caps inside. A GREAT GUM! A GREAT BANK!"

Bubble Calculator

Category: Miscellaneous
Contents: Gum, 15 sticks
Size: 1"h, 4"w, 4¾"d
Made for: Amurol Confection Co., Yorkville, IL 60560
Made in: U.S.A.
Cost new: $2.38 \ **Value:** $3.00 – 4.00
Description: Has a real calculator on the container. Front label reads "Bubble Calculator, fruit bubble gum 15 sticks — S'cool Bites fun x fun x fun x fun." Made in 1995.

Bubble Cube

Category: Games
Contents: Gum, 1.75 oz.
Size: 2½"h, 2½"w, 2½"d
Made for: Amurol Confections Co., Yorkville, IL 60560
Made in: U.S.A.
Value: $2.50 – 3.50
Description: 3D bubble gum puzzle. Has three levels for little gumballs. Made in 1994.

Bubble Fax (Iron Man)

Category: Games
Contents: Gum, 1.8 oz.
Size: 4⁹⁄₁₆"h, 2⅞"w, 1⅝"d
Made for: Classic Heroes Inc., Stuart, FL 34995
Made in: China
Value: $2.50 – 3.50
Description: Toy fax machine based on Iron Man superhero from Marvel Comics. Made in 1995. To make impression, place gum in tray, close lid and press. To change image, snap impression plate out of lid and turn over.

Bubble Jackpot

Category: Miscellaneous
Contents: Gum, 1.6 oz.
Size: 3⅝"h, 3⅛"w, 1"d
Made for: Amurol Confections Co., Yorkville, IL 60560
Made in: U.S.A.
Cost new: $.095 \ **Value:** $2.50 – $3.50
Description: Paper label looks like the front of a slot machine. © 1995.

Bubble Lock

Category: Miscellaneous
Contents: Gum, 1.23 oz.
Size: 4¼"h, 2¹³⁄₁₆"w, 1⅜"d
Made in: U.S.A.
Cost new: $0.95 \ **Value:** $1.50 – 3.00
Description: Toy combination lock filled with bubble gum. Dial turns, but lock doesn't work.

Bubble Tape

Category: Miscellaneous
Contents: Bubble gum, 2 oz.
Size: 3"h, 1"d
Made for: Amurol Confection Co., Yorkville, IL 60560
Made in: U.S.A.
Cost new: $1.19 \ **Value:** $1.19 – 2.25
Description: Made like a measuring tape. © 1997 Amurol Confection Co.

Bubblegum Fever

Category: Miscellaneous
Contents: Gum, 1.6 oz.
Size: 4¾"h, 3"w, ⅞"d
Made for: Zeebs Enterprises Inc., Ft. Worth, TX 76118
Made in: U.S.A.
Value: $3.50 – 5.00
Description: Outside cover made of paper. Inside is candy videocassette, with "BHS Video" gum embossed on it. Gum has BHS-Zeebs pressed into it, plus two holes to look like cassette.

Bucket (chalk)

Category: Miscellaneous
Contents: Gum, 3.5 oz.
Size: 2½"h, 2¾"w
Made for: The Foreign Candy Co., Hull, IA 51239
Made in: Mexico
Value: $2.50 – 3.50
Description: Paper label reads "Sidewalk Chalk bubble gum." Contains 11 chalk-like sticks of gum, in different colors.

Bug City

Category: Bottles and jars
Contents: Tarts, 2.6 oz.
Size: 2⅞"h, 2⅜"w
Made for: Amurol Confection Co., Yorkville, IL 60560
Made in: U.S.A.
Cost new: $0.99 \ **Value:** $1.50 – 2.00
Description: Has holes on top for air, when used for bugs. Paper label reads "Bug City – Candy Tarts – Reusable Bug Jar!" Made in 1992.

Bugs Bunny (pocket pack)

Category: Gumball dispenser
Contents: Gumballs
Size: 3½"h, 2³⁄₁₆"w, 1⅝"d
Made for: Processed Plastic Co., Montgomery, IL 60538
Made in: China
Value: $4.50 – 5.50
Description: A Tim Mee Toy, ™ & © 1989 Warner Bros., Inc. Bugs stands next to a stump, with one hand on it and the other holding a carrot. His legs are crossed. Lift Bugs Bunny's arm to dispense gumballs. Return arm to cover the opening. Gumball Pocket Pack Dispenser No. 5047.

Bus (Route 711)

Category: Transportation
Contents: Colored candy beads
Size: 1⅞"h, 1¹⁄₁₆"w, 3¾"d
Made for: Allen Mitchell Products
Made in: Hong Kong
Value: $14.00 – 18.00
Description: It has six windows on the side, two on the back, and one in front, on the top half of the bus. On the bottom there are five windows on the right side and three on the left, two in back, and one in front. The right side has two double doors and the left side has one single door. The paper labels read "D.D. Bus from Funsville America to Sweet Time U.S.A." and "Route 711." Embossed on the bottom: "Made in Hong Kong" and a star shaped mark for Allen Mitchell.

Bus (school)

Category: Nonplastic
Contents: Assorted hard candy, 6 oz.
Size: 4"h, 3⅛"w, 7"d
Made for: Springwater Enterprises, Springboro, OH 45066
Made in: Mexico
Cost new: $4.00 \ **Value:** $4.00 – 5.50
Description: Container is made of tin. Wheels rotate. Has No. 22 on the right side. Also has a coin slot on top, to be used as a bank. Purchased in 1997.

Buster Bunny

Category: Characters
Contents: Sugarless candy, 0.2 oz.
Size: 3¼"h, 2⅛"w, 1½"d
Made for: Topps Co., Duryea, PA 18642
Made in: China
Cost new: $0.99 \ **Value:** $3.50 – 5.00
Description: Head only. Top label reads "Tiny Toon Adventures." Licensed by Warner Bros. ™ & © 1991.

Buzz Lightyear (Toy Story 2)

Category: Characters
Contents: Nerds
Size: 6⅛"h, 4"w, 3"d
Made for: McDonald's Corp., Oak Brook, IL 60521
Made in: China
Cost new: $2.50 \ **Value:** $3.00 – 5.00
Description: Embossed on his bottom is "Mfg. for McD Corp. China/Chine MT 04 © 1999 McDonald's Corp. © Disney." Comes with a box of Wonka Nerds. 1.5 oz. This is also a wind-up toy. One in a series of six.

C-3PO (Europe)

Category: Characters
Contents: Candy Star Wars characters
Size: 2³⁄₁₆"h, 1½"w, 1⅝"d
Made for: Topps Ireland Ltd., Ballincollig Co.
Made in: China
Value: $5.00 – 6.50
Description: This Star Wars candy container was only released in Europe. It comes in a bag with a trading card.

C-3PO (head)

Category: Characters
Contents: Candy, 0.7 oz.
Size: 2½"h, 1½"w, 1½"d
Made for: Topps Co., Duryea, PA 18642
Made in: Hong Kong
Value: $4.50 – 6.50
Description: Embossed on the closure: "Star Wars – The Empire Strikes Back." Embossed on back of the head: "© 1980 LFL." To get candy out, turn closure to hole in the container.

CD 2000 (Galaxy Hotel)

Category: Transportation
Contents: Powdered candy
Size: 2¾"h, 1¾"w
Made for: Ce De Candy Inc., Union, NJ 07083
Made in: U.S.A.
Value: $4.00 – 6.00
Description: Tag reads "CD 2000 – candy-filled SPACE FLEET." Other side says "Really Dock!" "After you have enjoyed the candy, remove cap for extra docking port. Build a Space Complex. Command your own star squadron! Collect 'em, trade 'em. Keep the galaxy safe for (candy-loving) astronauts everywhere." Embossed on rim: "The Galaxy Hotel © CE DE 81."

CD 2000 (Orion Module)

Category: Transportation
Contents: Powdered candy
Size: 2¾"h, 1⁷⁄₁₆"w
Made for: Ce De Candy Inc., Union, NJ 07083
Made in: U.S.A.
Value: $4.00 – 6.00
Description: Part of series of Space Fleet containers. Tag reads "CD 2000 – candy filled SPACE FLEET." Embossed on the container: "© CE DE 81."

CD 2000 (Procyon Cruiser)

Category: Transportation
Contents: Powered candy
Size: 1¹⁄₁₆"h, 1³⁄₁₆"w, 3⅞"d
Made for: Ce De Candy, Inc., Union, NJ 07083
Made in: U.S.A.
Value: $4.00 – 6.00
Description: Part of series of Space Fleet containers. Tag reads "CD 2000 – candy filled SPACE FLEET." Embossed on container: "© CE DE 81 PROCYON CRUISER."

CD 2000 (Spaceport)

Category: Transportation
Contents: Powdered candy
Size: 2¾"h, 1¾"w ,1⁷⁄₁₆"d
Made for: Ce De Candy Inc., Union, NJ 07083
Made in: U.S.A.
Value: $4.00 – 6.00
Description: Another in a series of Space Fleet docking containers. Embossed on the container: "© CE DE 81."

CD Player

Category: Miscellaneous
Contents: Gum, 1.24 oz.
Size: ⅞"h, 3⅛"w, 4"d
Made for: Amurol Confections Co., Yorkville, IL 60560
Made in: U.S.A.
Cost new: $0.69 \ **Value:** $2.00 – 2.50
Description: Contains eight discs of bubble gum. Made in 1994.

CDs

Category: Miscellaneous
Contents: Gum, 1.4 oz.
Size: 4⅞"h, 5⅝"w, ⅜"d
Made for: Zeebs Enterprises Inc., Ft. Worth, TX 76118
Made in: U.S.A.
Cost new: $1.68 \ **Value:** $3.00 – 4.00
Description: Came in many titles, such as Santa Busts Loose, Holly Jolly Jam Band, De Frosty, Rude-Elf, McSloppy Hog & DJ Doogie, Catman, Mighty Mutant Power Turtles, Crooks & Gumm, Chew B 40, Gums-N-JP Josers, Bubblin' Stones, and Saltin'Pep O Ment.

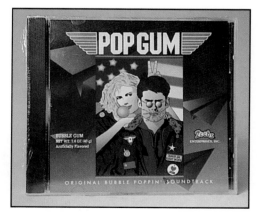

Camera (Candy)

Category: Battery operated
Contents: Sweet Tarts, 1 oz.
Size: 3"h, 4⅝"w, 1⅛"d
Made for: Tapper Candy Inc., Cleveland, OH 44146
Made in: China
Value: $3.00 – 4.50
Description: Light comes on when you press button. Has blue vinyl cord coming out left side. © 1996. Comes in other colors.

Camera (Pooh)

Category: Battery operated
Contents: Sweet Tarts
Size: 3½"h, 4¾"w, 1⁵⁄₁₆"d
Made for: Tapper Candy Inc., Cleveland, OH 44146
Made in: China
Value: $4.00 – 6.00
Description: Embossed on the back lower right: "© Tapper Candies, Inc. © Disney." The light comes on when you press the button. This container came on a card. Net Wt. 0.32 oz.

Camera (Hot Flash)

Category: Miscellaneous
Contents: Gum, 0.85 oz.
Size: 1⅞"h, 2¾"w, 1⁹⁄₁₆"d
Made for: Donruss Co., Memphis, TN 38101
Value: $6.50 – 8.50
Description: Lens is closure. Embossed on front of camera above lens: "Hot Flash."

Canadian Avalanche

Category: Bottles and jars
Contents: Gum
Size: 3¾"h, 1⅜"w, 1⅛"d
Value: $2.00 – 3.00
Description: Purchased in Yuma, Arizona, in 1995. Has "Canadian Avalanche" on the label and that is all. Probably made in Mexico.

Can-D-Sip

Category: Food items
Contents: Orange fruit juice powder, 0.35 oz.
Size: 2"h, 1 1/16"w
Made for: Allen Mitchell Products, Oxnard, CA 93030
Made in: Malaysia
Cost new: $0.49 \ **Value:** $1.00 – 1.50
Description: Comes with a straw. Add water to make orange drink. Not for children under 3.

Candy Bloomer

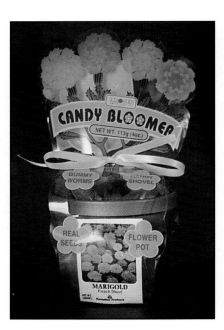

Category: Miscellaneous
Contents: Gummi worms
Size: 4 1/4"w, 3 5/8"h (container), total height 9 1/4"
Made for: E. Rosen Co., Pawtucket, RI 02860
Made in: China
Value: $2.50 – 3.50
Description: Has real marigold seeds and small, yellow plastic shovel. Container doubles as flowerpot. Small pack of seeds in front. Yellow ribbon holds plastic covering.

Candy Bubbles (cotton candy)

Category: Battery operated
Contents: Liquid candy, 2 oz.
Size: 7 5/16"h, 2 1/4"w, 1 13/16"d
Made for: Cap Toys Inc., Bedford Heights, OH 44146
Made in: China
Value: $2.00 – 3.00
Description: Front of label reads "Cotton candy-candy bubbles. Bubbles you can eat!" Back label reads "Important: novelty item, not a food product. Bubbles safe for consumption. Liquid not to be consumed." Button on the back operates. © 1995.

Candy Bubbles (jar)

Category: Bottles and jars
Contents: Liquid candy
Size: 4 1/4"h, 1 13/16"w
Made for: Cap Toys Inc., Bedford Heights, OH 44146
Made in: U.S.A.
Value: $1.00 – 1.50
Description: Label reads "Candy Bubbles – Bubbles you can eat! Artificial Flavor GRAPE. Important: Novelty item. Not a food product. Bubbles safe for consumption. Liquid not intended to be consumed." Has plastic a loop inside. © 1995.

Candy Crane

Category: Games
Contents: Gumballs, 1.25 oz.
Size: 5⅜"h, 3⅞"w, 4¾"d
Made for: Bee International, Chula Vista, CA 91912
Made in: China
Value: $6.50 – 8.50
Description: To get a gumball you pick one up and bring it over to the hole and drop it. Instructions are on the bottom.

Candy Handler (M&M's minis)

Category: Characters
Contents: M&M's minis, 1.24 oz.
Size: 4⅜"h, 5¼"w, 1¼"d
Made for: OddzOn/Cap Toys, Inc., Bedford Hts, OH 44146
Made in: China
Cost new: $3.99 \ **Value:** $4.00 – 5.50
Description: The candy is removed from the container by pushing the left hand down. The right hand moves in and gets a piece of candy. Comes on a card with M&M's Minis.

Candy Jug

Category: Bottles and jars
Contents: Candy, 1.4 oz.
Size: 3⁹⁄₁₆"h, 2½"w, 1¼"d
Made for: Amurol Products Co., Naperville, IL 60566
Made in: U.S.A.
Cost new: $0.69 \ **Value:** $1.00 – 1.50
Description: Paper label on the front reads "Shake & Chug – Cookies & Cream – Candy Jug." Screw top. Embossed on the bottom: "61313 HOPE 6."

Candy Kitchen

Category: Holidays
Contents: Milk chocolate, 3 oz.
Size: 6"h, 3¼"w, 3¼"d
Made for: Russell Stover Candies, Kansas City, MO 64106
Made in: China
Cost new: $4.99 \ **Value:** $6.00 – 8.00
Description: Little house with Santa Claus at front door and elves in windows and on roof. Mrs. Claus putting present in sack. Reindeer at back door. Inside are 12 foil-wrapped milk chocolate Santas. Has coin slot to be used as a bank. Embossed on bottom: "© 1996 Determined Productions Inc. Made in China 1-2."

Candy Kitchen (Bugs Bunny)

Category: Holidays
Contents: Milk chocolate, 3 oz.
Size: 5⅛"h, 3⅝"w, 3⁹⁄₁₆"d
Made for: Russell Stover Candies, Kansas City, MO 64106
Made in: China
Cost new: $4.99 \ **Value:** $6.00 – 7.00
Description: House is also a bank. In windows are Looney Tunes characters. Characters also featured on candy foil wrappers. Made in 1997.

Candy Pager

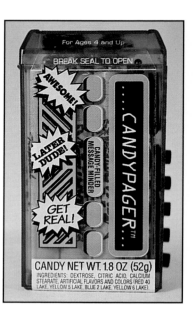

Category: Battery operated
Contents: Tropical Smarties, 1.8 oz.
Size: 3¹³⁄₁₆"h, 2⅛"w, 1½"d
Made for: Berzerk Candy Werks, Memphis, TN 38119
Made in: China
Cost new: $1.69 \ **Value:** $3.00 – 4.50
Description: Battery operated. Makes four different sounds: beep, awesome, later dude, and get real. Came with a belt clip. Made in 1994.

Candy Pendants

Category: Miscellaneous
Contents: Small colored nuggets
Size: 2⅝"h, 2"w, ¾"d
Made for: Imperial Toy Corporation, Los Angeles, CA 90021
Made in: China
Cost new: $1.50 \ **Value:** $2.50 – 3.00
Description: Comes on a card that reads "Candy Pendants – Candy Club – filled with WillyWonka's Nerds – © The WillyWonka Candy Factory, Division of Sunmark Inc."

Candy Popper

Category: Battery operated
Contents: Candy pellets, 1.4 oz.
Size: 6¾"h, 2⅝"w, 2⁵⁄₁₆"d
Made for: Cap Toys Inc., Bedford Heights, OH 44146
Made in: China
Cost new: $2.29 \ **Value:** $3.00 – 4.00
Description: Battery operated. Has button in front to press. Candy jumps around and comes out the side. Paper stick on yellow label reads "Press Here — Candy Popper — Refill with any small hard candy!" No. 4720. © 1995.

Candy Store

Category: Nonplastic
Contents: Chocolate candy, 2 oz.
Size: 3¼"h, 3"w, 1½"d
Made for: R.M. Palmer Co., West Reading, PA 19611
Cost new: $0.79 \ Value: $3.50 – 4.50
Description: This container is made of paper. It has a punch out spot on the roof to put a string in to be used as a Christmas ornament. There are others in this series.

Candy Tumbler

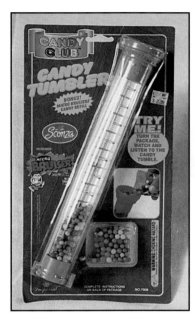

Category: Miscellaneous
Contents: Micro bruiser jaw breakers
Size: 11⅜"h, 1⅞"w
Made for: Imperial Toy Corporation, Los Angeles, CA 90021
Made in: China
Cost new: $2.99 \ Value: $3.00 – 4.00
Description: Comes on a card with extra candy. Card reads "Candy Club TM. NO.7008 Candy made in U.S.A. – Tumbler made in China – Packaging made and printed in Hong Kong." Embossed near the top: "Candy Club™," on the bottom: "Imperial © 1997 made in China."

Cannon

Category: Miscellaneous
Contents: Small colored candy balls
Size: 1"h, ¾"w, 2⅜"d
Made in: West Germany
Value: $5.50 – 7.00
Description: Barrel has "WEST GERMANY" embossed on it.

Car (#35)

Category: Transportation
Contents: Smarties, 3 oz.
Size: 2"h, 2⅞"w, 7⅜"d
Made for: Hilo Corp., Norristown, PA 19401
Made in: China
Cost new: $1.49 \ Value: $3.00 – 4.00
Description: Sports car (No. 35) doubles as a bank. Label covers coin slot. Screw closure at rear of the car. © 1994. Comes in other colors.

Car (Batmobile)

Category: Transportation
Contents: Candy, 0.25 oz.
Size: ¾"h, 1⁹⁄₁₆"w, 3¾"d
Made for: Topps Co. Inc., Duryea, PA 18642
Made in: China
Cost new: $0.49 \ **Value:** $5.00 – 7.00
Description: All black except for white Batman insignia on top. Wheels rotate. © 1991.

Car (Flintstones)

Category: Transportation
Contents: Candy, 0.4 oz.
Size: 1⅞"h, 2⅛"w, 3⁵⁄₁₆"d
Made for: Topps Co., Duryea, PA 18642
Made in: China
Cost new: $0.59 \ **Value:** $4.00 – 6.00
Description: Flintstones car with Fred and Dino. © 1993.

Car (racer)

Category: Transportation
Contents: Colored candy beads, 0.15 oz.
Size: 1½"h, 2⅛"w, 4⁵⁄₁₆"d
Made for: Allen Mitchell Products, Oxnard, CA 93030
Made in: Malaysia
Value: $4.00 – 5.00
Description: Comes in different colors and numbers. Wrapped in plastic.

Car (small race car)

Category: Transportation
Contents: Colored gum bits
Size: 1"h, ¹⁵⁄₁₆"w, 2¾"d
Value: $1.50 – 2.00
Description: There is a number "1" on the hood of the car. No other markings are on the container. Made of soft plastic.

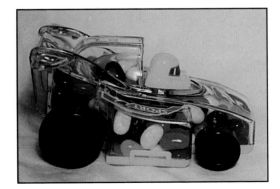

Car (Sports 3)

Category: Transportation
Contents: Candy jelly beans
Size: 2⅜"h, 3¼"w, 5"d
Made for: Rocky Mountain Chocolate Factory, Atascadero, CA
Made in: China
Cost new: $6.75 \ **Value:** $6.00 – 8.00
Description: Came wrapped in clear plastic bag with yellow ribbon. Embossed on bottom: "MADE IN CHINA U.K.D. 1042068 P.R.C.D. 87301350.6."

Car (Turbo Racer)

Category: Transportation
Contents: Tart candy rolls, 1.5 oz.
Size: 2¹⁵⁄₁₆"h, 3½"w, 5⅝"d
Made for: The Jelly Bean Factory, Fairfax, OH 45227
Made in: China
Cost new: $1.97 \ **Value:** $2.00 – 3.50
Description: Came in different colors, with different numbers. Sticker reads "Turbo #7." Has a coin slot. Sticker says "BANK."

Carrot Patch

Category: Food items
Contents: Gum, 1.7 oz.
Size: 6¼"h, 1¾"w
Made for: Creative Confection Concepts, Milwaukee, WI 53209
Made in: Mexico
Cost new: $1.49 \ **Value:** $4.50 – 7.00
Description: Bugs Bunny product. Has a plastic cord, to be worn around the neck. Carrot has three teeth marks. Front label reads "Bugs Bunny Carrot Patch." In cartoon, Bugs is saying "What's up Doc?" and "It's Bubble Gum!" © 1996.

Casper (head)

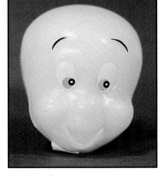

Category: Characters
Contents: Gum
Size: 2¹⁵⁄₁₆"h, 1¹³⁄₁₆"w, 2"d
Made for: Topps Co., Duryea, PA 18642
Made in: China
Cost new: $1.29 \ **Value:** $3.00 – 4.00
Description: Casper's head glows in the dark. Part of a series of four: Casper and ghostly friends. Embossed on back: "Casper © 1995 UCS and Amblin.™ Harvey."

Cat (Candy Pet)

Category: Animals
Contents: Candy colored beads
Size: 2¾"h, 1¾"w, 1½"d
Made for: Wizard Toys Inc., Bell, CA 90201
Made in: China
Value: $3.00 – 4.00
Description: There are six different Wizard Candy Pets: Bear, Cat, Chick, Dog, Duck, and Pig. They are sold on a card. Net Wt. 1 oz. The hat is the closure. Candy made in Canada. Item 7100.

Cat (Stimpy, Nickelodeon)

Category: Animals
Contents: Gum, 0.4 oz.
Size: 2³⁄₁₆"h, 1¹³⁄₁₆"w, 2"d
Made for: Topps Co., Duryea, PA 18642
Made in: China
Value: $4.50 – 6.00
Description: Another in the Nickelodeon container series. Head only. Has tongue hanging out left side of his mouth. Embossed on back: "© 1993 NICKELODEON."

Cat (Tom)

Category: Characters
Contents: Pill-shaped candy
Size: 3⅞"h, 2⁵⁄₁₆"w, 1⁵⁄₁₆"d
Made for: Bee International, Chula Vista, CA 91912
Made in: China
Value: $7.00 – 8.00
Description: This is Tom from the characters Tom & Jerry. The label on the container reads "© 1993 T.E.C. & Telefilm-Essen Gmbh. All Rights Reserved." Tom & Jerry The Movie™ are trademarks of Turner Entertainment Co. The candy has the name Tom on some and Jerry on the others. Embossed on the back of the head is "© 1993 T.E.C."

Checkbook

Category: Miscellaneous
Contents: Gum, 2 oz.
Size: ½"h, 5¹³⁄₁₆"w, 2½"d
Made for: Amurol Confections Co., Naperville, IL 60567-2286
Made in: U.S.A.
Cost new: $1.00 \ **Value:** $1.00 – 1.50
Description: Came in different colors. Made of vinyl or cardboard. Inside is the same. Label reads "April 1, 1999 – I. M. Rich – 1,000,000 – One Million Dollars and 00/100 – Bo Gus Bucks." © 1994.

Chew Fun (carryout box)

Category: Nonplastic
Contents: Gum, 0.4oz.
Size: 2⅝"h, 1¾"w, 1½"d
Made for: The Topps Co., Duryea, PA 18642
Made in: Hong Kong
Value: $5.00 – 8.00
Description: Looks like food from a Chinese restaurant. The bubble gum inside looks like noodles. © 1985. Paper box with a plastic handle.

Chewbacca (Europe)

Category: Characters
Contents: Candy Star Wars characters
Size: 2¼"h, 1½"w, 1⅜"d
Made for: Topps Ireland Ltd., Ballincollig Co.
Made in: China
Value: $5.00 – 6.50
Description: This Star Wars candy container was only released in Europe. It comes in a bag with a trading card.

Chick (bank)

Category: Animals
Contents: Speckled candy eggs, 2 oz.
Size: 4"h, 2⅝"w, 2¹¹⁄₁₆"d
Made for: Hilco Corp., Norristown, PA 19401
Made in: China
Cost new: $0.99 \ **Value:** $3.00 – 4.00
Description: Paper stick-ons for eyes. Doubles as a bank. Embossed on the bottom: "© 1991 Hilco Corp China."

Chick (Candy Pet)

Category: Animals
Contents: Colored candy beads
Size: 2¾"h, 1¾"w, 1⅝"d
Made for: Wizard Toys Inc., Bell, CA 90201
Made in: China
Value: $3.00 – 4.00
Description: There are six different Wizard Candy Pets: Bear, Cat, Chick, Dog, Duck, and Pig. They are sold on a card. Net Wt. 1 oz. The hat is the closure. Candy made in Canada. Item 7100.

Chick in Egg

Category: Animals
Contents: Colored round candy, 2.1 oz.
Size: 5⅝"h, 1⅞"w, 2⅛"d
Made for: R.L. Albert & Son, Inc., Greenwich, CT 06830
Made in: China
Cost new: $1.29 \ **Value:** $2.50 – 3.50
Description: Tag reads "Baby Chick Eggs. Candy filled eggs." It has a plastic hook on the top so it can be hung as an ornament.

Chick with Hat

Category: Animals
Contents: Candy jelly eggs, 7 oz.
Size: 6"h, 3½"w
Made for: Hilco Corp., Norris Town, PA 19401
Made in: China
Cost new: $2.99 \ **Value:** $4.00 – 6.00
Description: This chick is in a half egg, and is wearing a hat. The hat has a coin slot to be used as a bank. Paper stickers for eyes.

Christmas Tree

Category: Nonplastic
Contents: Candy
Size: 5⅜"h, 4¼"w, 1⅝"d
Made for: Hershey Foods Corp., Hershey, PA 17033-0810
Made in: China
Value: $3.00 – 4.00
Description: Made of paper. Part of Hershey's Holiday Collectible series. This is number 1. © 1995.

Christmas Tree (Holiday Greetings)

Category: Holidays
Contents: Colored candy, 1 oz.
Size: 3⅛"h, 2¹⁵⁄₁₆"w, ⅞"d
Made for: E. Rosen Company, Pawtucket, RI 02860
Value: $2.00 – 3.50
Description: The star on top of the tree has eight dots around it. Container was designed to double as a Christmas tree ornament. There are no markings on the container.

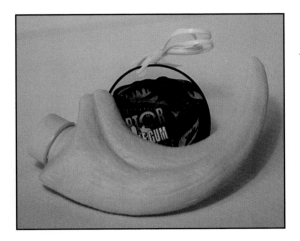

Claw (raptor)

Category: Animals
Contents: Bubble gum powders, 1.7 oz.
Size: 7"h (through the center), 2½"w, 1¼"d
Made for: Creative Confection Concepts, Milwaukee, WI 53209
Made in: Mexico
Cost new: $1.29 \ **Value:** $5.00 – 7.50
Description: Closure is screw top with no seal. Comes with plastic lacing and tag featuring picture of a raptor dinosaur. Embossed on the side: "CCC LLC Made in Mexico."

Clown (black hat)

Category: Characters
Contents: Candy
Size: 7½"h, 2¹⁵⁄₁₆"w, 2⅜"d
Made in: Hong Kong
Value: $11.00 – 15.00
Description: Embossed on the back is "Hong Kong." It has a money slot in the back. This was also used as a bank.

Clown (Kandy Andy)

Category: Characters
Contents: Candy
Size: 8"h, 2⅞"w, 2¼"d
Made for: E. Rosen Co., Pawtucket, RI 02862
Made in: Hong Kong
Value: $9.00 – 12.00
Description: Embossed on the back of the head is "Kong Hong." They spelled it that way. Also found without any markings. The same body was used with different heads.

Coffin (Mr. Bones)

Category: Miscellaneous
Contents: Candy, 0.35 oz.
Size: 1¹⁄₁₆"h, 1⁷⁄₁₆"w, 3³⁄₁₆"d
Made for: Fleer Corp., Philadelphia, PA 19141
Made in: U.S.A.
Cost new: $0.49 \ **Value:** $3.00 – 4.00
Description: Shaped like a coffin. Came in many colors. Has "Mr. Bones" embossed on top. Ring for hanging.

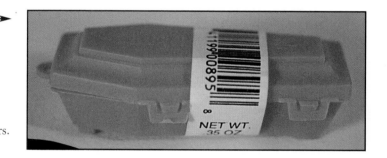

Coffin (skeleton)

Category: Miscellaneous
Contents: Candy, 0.95 oz.
Size: 4"h, 2⅜"w, 1"d
Made for: R.L. Albert & Son, Greenwich, CT 06830
Made in: China
Value: $2.50 – 3.50
Description: Has glow-in-dark skeleton on top and skeleton embossed on bottom. Candies inside are shaped like skeleton parts.

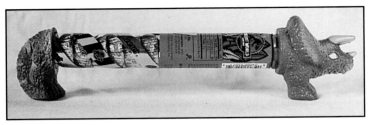

Collectable Connectables
(blue dinosaur, Lost World)

Category: Animals
Contents: Peanut butter cups, 2.7 oz.
Size: 3"h, 2¼"w, 12"d
Made for: H.B. Reese Candy Co., Hershey, PA 17033-8015
Made in: China
Cost new: $2.29 \ **Value:** $3.50 – 4.50
Description: Part of a series of connectable animal and dinosaur containers from the movie "Lost World." Embossed on the head: "MADE IN CHINA B3-P™ & © 1997 UCS & AMBLIN HC USA."

Collectable Connectables
(green dinosaur)

Category: Animals
Contents: Peanut butter cups, 2.7 oz.
Size: 2¼"h, 1¹¹⁄₁₆"w, 10¾"d
Made for: H.B. Reese Candy Co., Hershey, PA 17033-0815
Made in: China
Cost new: $2.29 \ **Value:** $3.50 – 4.50
Description: Part of interchangeable series of containers. Embossed on the head: "MADE IN CHIA B2-P™ & © 1997 UCS & AMBLIN HC USA." Same on the back leg.

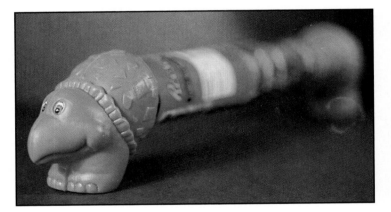

Collectable Connectables
(green dinosaur, Lost World)

Category: Animals
Contents: Peanut butter cups, 2.7 oz.
Size: 2¹⁵⁄₁₆"h, 1⅝"w, 11¾"d
Made for: H.B. Reese Candy Co., Hershey, PA 17033-0815
Made in: China
Cost new: $2.29 \ **Value:** $3.50 – 4.50
Description: Part of a series of dinosaur containers, "Lost World," which can link together. Embossed on the head: "MADE IN CHINA B2-P™ & © 1997 UCS & AMBLIN HC USA."

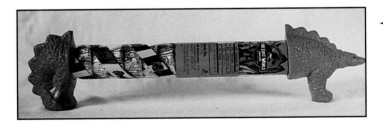

Collectable Connectables (orange fish)

Category: Animals
Contents: Peanut butter cups, 2.7 oz.
Size: 2½"h, 2"w, 11¼"d
Made for: H.B. Reese Co., Hershey, PA 17033-0815
Made in: China
Cost new: $2.29 \ **Value:** $3.50 – 4.50
Description: Part of interchangeable series. Embossed on the head and tail: "HERSHEY FOODS CHINA B2."

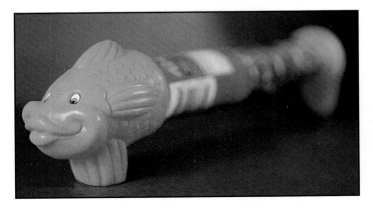

Collectable Connectables
(purple dinosaur)

Category: Animals
Contents: Peanut butter cups, 2.7 oz.
Size: 2⁹⁄₁₆"h, 1⅝"w, 11¼"d
Made for: H.B. Reese Candy Co., Hershey, PA 17011-0815
Made in: China
Cost new: $2.29 \ **Value:** $3.50 – 4.50
Description: Part of a series of dinosaurs that can connect to form strange-looking creatures. Embossed on the head, left side: "HERSHEY FOODS." Embossed on the right side: "CHINA B2." © 1997.

Collectable Connectables
(yellow lion)

Category: Animals
Contents: Peanut butter cups, 2.7 oz.
Size: 2¾"h, 2"w, 11½"d
Made for: H.B. Reese Co., Hershey, PA 17033-0815
Made in: China
Cost new: $2.29 \ **Value:** $3.50 – 4.50
Description: Part of a series of animal and dinosaur containers that are connectable. Embossed on both ends: "HERSHEY FOODS CHINA B2." © 1997.

Cookie Jar (rectangular)

Category: Bottles and jars
Contents: Pressed-sugar, 0.4 oz.
Size: 2"h, 1¼"w, 1¼"d
Made for: Concord Confections Inc., Ontario, Canada
Made in: Canada
Cost new: $0.59 \ **Value:** $2.50 – 3.50
Description: Rectangular, with two squares of different size on top. Embossed on the bottom: "© Concord Confections Inc."

Cookie Jar (round)

Category: Bottles and jars
Contents: Candy, 0.4 oz.
Size: 1¹⁵⁄₁₆"h, 1⁹⁄₁₆"w
Made for: Concord Confections Inc., Ontario, Canada
Made in: Canada
Cost new: $0.59 \ **Value:** $2.50 – 3.50
Description: Shaped like a cylinder, with bear's face on top. Embossed on the bottom: "© Concord Confections Inc."

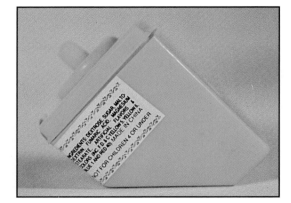

Cookie Jar (slanted)

Category: Bottles and jars
Contents: Candy, 0.4 oz.
Size: 1⅝"h, 1⅛"w, 2¼"d
Made for: Concord Confections Inc., Ontario, Canada
Made in: Canada
Cost new: $0.59 \ **Value:** $2.50 – 3.50
Description: Looks like an old-time mercantile jar. Embossed on the back: "© Concord Confections Inc."

Corn (popcorn, Foghorn Leghorn)

Category: Food items
Contents: Gum, 1.5 oz.
Size: 6¾"h, 1⅝"w, 2"d
Made for: Creative Confection Concepts, Milwaukee, WI 53209
Made in: Mexico
Cost new: $1.49 \ **Value:** $5.50 – 8.00
Description: Featuring Foghorn Leghorn, the Warner Brothers cartoon rooster. Has a plastic cord. Can be worn around the neck. Screw-on closure. Label reads "Foghorn Leghorn – Popcorn-flavored bubble gum." Embossed on the side: "made in Mexico™ & © 1996 Warner Bros."

Crayon (bank)

Category: Crayons, pencils, and pens
Contents: Jelly beans
Size: 6⅜"h, 1⅛"w
Made for: Ralphco Inc., 50 Gardner, Worcester, MA 01610
Made in: U.S.A.
Cost new: $0.99 \ **Value:** $2.00 – 3.00
Description: Has coin slot for bank.

Crayon (Scribbles)

Category: Crayons, pencils, and pens
Contents: Fruit-shaped Runts, 2.25 oz.
Size: 10⅜"h, 1¹⁄₁₆"w
Made for: Bee International, Chula Vista, CA 91914
Cost new: $1.00 \ **Value:** $1.50 – 2.50
Description: Crayon tip that really writes. Embossed on bottom: "BEE CA 90040."

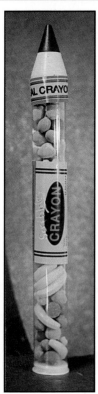

Crayon (Tangerine)

Category: Crayons, pencils, and pens
Contents: Candy paste, 1.23 oz.
Size: 3¾"h, 1½"w
Made for: Lorena Mexican Products Inc., Otay Mesa, CA 92173
Made in: Mexico
Cost new: $0.45 \ **Value:** $1.50 – 2.50
Description: Has a soft tip. Purchased in Yuma, Arizona, in 1997. Same as Crayon Pop with a different label and made for different company.

Crayon (Tart-n-Tinys)

Category: Crayons, pencils, and pens
Contents: Red, white, and pink candy hearts
Size: 7"h, 1⅛"w
Made for: Sunmark Inc., St. Louis, MO
Made in: U.S.A.
Cost new: $1.49 \ **Value:** $3.00 – 4.00
Description: Label says "Crayon-Bank," but there is no coin slot. Tip is a ballpoint pen. © 1994.

Crayon Pop

Category: Crayons, pencils, and pens
Contents: Gum, 1.1 oz.
Size: 3¾"h, 1½"w
Made for: Phila Chewing Gum Corp., Havertown, PA 19038
Made in: Mexico
Cost new: $0.69 \ **Value:** $1.50 – 2.00
Description: Same as Crayon (Tangerine) with different label. For children 4 and under. This one is tangerine-flavored, too.

Crayons

Category: Crayons, pencils, and pens
Contents: Jelly beans, 2 oz.
Size: 6⅜"h, 1"w
Made for: Horizon Creations, Pacoima, CA
Cost new: $0.59 \ **Value:** $1.50 – 2.00
Description: All clear plastic except for two white stripes on top and bottom.

Crayons (coin bank, large)

Category: Crayons, pencils, and pens
Contents: Jaw breakers
Size: 7¼"h, 2⅛"w
Made for: Horizon Candy, El Paso, TX 79906
Made in: Tube in U.S.A.; top and base in Taiwan
Cost new: $1.50 \ **Value:** $1.50 – 2.00
Description: This also comes with super-sour bubblegum balls. Has a coin slot on top. Comes in different colors.

Cubby Bank

Category: Animals
Contents: Jelly beans, 8 oz.
Size: 6"h, 3¹³⁄₁₆"w, 3½"d
Made for: Hilco Corp., Norristown, PA 19401
Made in: Thailand (candy in U.S.A.)
Cost new: $2.50 \ **Value:** $4.00 – 5.00
Description: Bear sitting with top hat and bow tie. Tag is in shape of a heart that reads "Candy Filled Cubby Bank." Inside tag reads "Happy Valentine's Day." Slot in the hat for use as a bank.

Cup (dino)

Category: Miscellaneous
Contents: Smarties, 4 oz.
Size: 4"h, 2½"w, 3"d
Made for: Hilco Corp., Norristown, PA 19401
Made in: China
Cost new: $1.97 \ **Value:** $3.00 – 4.00
Description: This cup has no handle. Containers came with candy or gum. Has "DINO CUP" written on front of the cup, and raised picture of a dinosaur on top. Embossed on the bottom: "made in China – Hilco Corporation © 1993."

Cup (sunglasses)

Category: Miscellaneous
Contents: Gum, 3.5 oz.
Size: 4⅞"h, 3⁵⁄₁₆"w, 4"d
Made for: Hilco Corp., Norristown, PA 19401
Made in: Thailand
Cost new: $1.97 \ **Value:** $3.00 – 4.00
Description: Has two loops on the back for fingers. Embossed on the bottom: "made in Thailand – Hilco Corporation © 1993."

Daffy Duck

Category: Characters
Contents: Gumballs
Size: 3⅛"h, 2¼"w
Made for: Superior Toy & Manufacturing Co., Chicago, IL 60657
Made in: China; assembled in U.S.A.
Value: $5.50 – 6.50
Description: This is a Gumball Pocket Pack Dispenser. Daffy is standing in front of a star with a suitcase marked "gumballs" in his right hand. Open Daffy's suitcase to dispense gum. Close suitcase to cover opening. Daffy is wearing a yellow hat and coat with green tie. No. 5048. This may be only one in a series made for Superior Toy. Others made by Processed Plastic Co.

Darth Vader

Category: Characters
Contents: Candy pellets, 0.7 oz.
Size: 2½"h, 1¹¹⁄₁₆"w, 1¹¹⁄₁₆"d
Made for: The Topps Co., Duryea, PA 18642
Made in: Hong Kong
Value: $5.00 – 6.50
Description: Embossed on the closure: "Star Wars – The Empire Strikes Back." To get the candy out, you turn closure to hole in the container. Embossed on back of the head: "© 1980 LFL."

Darth Vader (Europe)

Category: Characters
Contents: Candy Star War characters
Size: 2⁵⁄₁₆"h, 1¹³⁄₁₆"w, 2"d
Made for: Topps Ireland Ltd., Ballincollig Co.
Made in: China
Value: $5.00 – 6.50
Description: This Star Wars candy container was only released in Europe. It comes in a bag with a trading card.

Deer (Rudolph, head)

Category: Animals
Contents: Candy and stickers
Size: 2¾"h, 2½"w, 1³⁄₁₆"d
Made in: China
Value: $3.50 – 5.00
Description: Closure is on the bottom. Can be hung as an ornament. Inside are small package of candy and two peel-off stickers. Rudolph has a red nose and tongue. Embossed on the bottom: "Made In China."

Diamond Ring

Category: Miscellaneous
Contents: Small colored candy balls, 0.53 oz.
Size: 3¼"h, 1⁹⁄₁₆"w
Made for: Goodlite Products Inc., Bedford, TX 76021
Made in: China
Cost new: $0.69 \ **Value:** $2.00 – 3.00
Description: Six-sided diamond with screw-top closure. Item No. FT20310.

Dino (Flintstones)

Category: Animals
Contents: Pill-shaped with pictures of Flintstones characters, 0.2 oz.
Size: 3¼"h, 1½"w, 1⁵⁄₁₆"d
Made for: Topps Co., Duryea, PA 18642
Made in: China
Cost new: $0.59 \ **Value:** $3.50 – 5.00
Description: Push-in closure on the bottom. Soft plastic comb on top of the head. © 1993, licensed by Universal Studios and Amblin Entertainment.

Dino Eggs (blue head)

Category: Animals
Contents: Blue raspberry powdered candy, 1.5 oz.
Size: 2¹⁵⁄₁₆"h, 2¹⁄₁₆"w, 4"d
Made for: Creative Confections Concepts, Milwaukee, WI 53209
Made in: Mexico
Cost new: $1.29 \ **Value:** $4.00 – 6.00
Description: Blue baby dinosaur head is breaking out of its shell. Head is also the closure. Part of series. Embossed on the side: "CCC LLC made in Mexico."

Dino Eggs (triceratops, red) →

Category: Animals
Contents: Strawberry powdered candy, 1.5 oz.
Size: 2⁵⁄₁₆"h, 2¹⁄₁₆"w, 4"d
Made for: Creative Confections Concepts, Milwaukee, WI 53209
Made in: Mexico
Cost new: $1.29 \ Value: $4.00 – 6.00
Description: Red baby triceratops is hatching. Head is also the closure. Embossed on the side: "CCC LLC made in Mexico."

← Dino Eggs (yellow head)

Category: Animals
Contents: Banana creme powdered candy, 1.5 oz.
Size: 2⁵⁄₁₆"h, 2¹⁄₁₆"w, 4"d
Made for: Creative Confections Concepts, Milwaukee, WI 53209
Made in: Mexico
Cost new: $1.29 \ **Value:** $4.00 – 6.00
Description: Yellow baby dinosaur is hatching. Head is the closure. Part of a series. Embossed on the side: "CCC LLC made in Mexico."

Dino Long Neck (Baby) →

Category: Animals
Contents: Colored candy pills, 0.4 oz.
Size: 2⅝"h, 1¼"w, 1⅝"d
Made for: The Topps Co. Inc., Duryea, PA 18642
Made in: Hong Kong
Value: $6.50 – 8.00
Description: Embossed on the side of the neck: "© 1985 Walt Disney Prods." From the movie "Baby."

← Dino Sitting (Baby, full body)

Category: Animals
Contents: Colored candy pills, 0.4oz.
Size: 2⅝"h, 1⅝"w, 1⁷⁄₁₆"d
Made for: The Topps Co. Inc., Duryea, PA 18642
Made in: Hong Kong
Value: $6.50 – 8.00
Description: Embossed on the back: "© 1985 Walt Disney Prods." The neck separates from the body to open. From the movie "Baby."

55

Dinosaur (Rex, Toy Story 2)

Category: Animals
Contents: Sweet Tarts
Size: 5¾"h, 4⅝"w, 5¼"d
Made for: McDonald's Corp., Oak Brook, IL 60521
Made in: China
Cost new: $2.50 \ **Value:** $3.00 – 5.00
Description: Embossed on the bottom is "Mfg. for McD Corp. China/Chine TF 01 © 1999 McDonald's Corp. © Disney – Disney/Pixar Toy Story 2." Candy Net Wt. 1.22 oz. The candy is deposited in the neck and you turn the head side to side to dispense the candy down the tail. One in a series of six.

Dinosaur Jurassic Park (head only)

Category: Animals
Contents: Gum, 0.4 oz.
Size: 1¹⁵⁄₁₆"h, 1⅞"w, 3¹⁄₁₆"d
Made for: Topps Co., Duryea, PA 18642
Made in: China
Value: $4.00 – 5.00
Description: Head mounted on rock wall. From the Jurassic Park movies.

Dinosaur Jurassic Park (long neck)

Category: Animals
Contents: Gum, 0.4 oz.
Size: 1¹⁵⁄₁₆"h, 1⅞"w, 2¹⁵⁄₁₆"d
Made for: Topps Co., Duryea, PA 18642
Made in: China
Value: $4.00 – 5.00
Description: A Jurassic Park container. Head and neck mounted on grass-covered rock wall.

Discovery

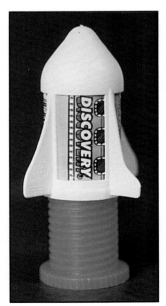

Category: Transportation
Contents: Candy paste, 25g
Size: 4⅛"h, 2½"w
Made for: Dulces
Made in: Mexico
Cost new: $0.35 \ **Value:** $2.50 – 3.00
Description: Container is vaguely shaped like a space shuttle. Embossed on the wings: "Jale," with an arrow pointing up. On the other side are American insignia and markings for flaps.

Dog (Candy Pet)

Category: Animals
Contents: Colored candy beads
Size: 2¾"h, 1¹³⁄₁₆"w, 1¾"d
Made for: Wizard Toys Inc., Bell, CA 90201
Made in: China
Value: $3.00 – 4.00
Description: There are six different Wizard Candy Pets: Bear, Cat, Chick, Dog, Duck, and Pig. They are sold on a card. Net Wt. 1 oz. The hat is the closure. Candy made in Canada. Item 7100.

Dog (Milo, Mask)

Category: Animals
Contents: Jaw breakers, 1.75 oz.
Size: 5⅜"h, 1⅝"w, 1⅞"d
Made for: Imagining 3, Niles, IL 60714
Made in: China
Value: $4.00 – 5.50
Description: Collectible candy machine dispensing jaw-breakers. From New Line Productions, © 1995. For ages 3 and up. Embossed on the bottom: "Patents Pending PATS 5,385,267 D359,232 made in China."

Dog (Ren, Nickelodeon)

Category: Animals
Contents: Gum, 0.4 oz.
Size: 2⅜"h, 2⅜"w, 2"d
Made for: Topps Co., Duryea, PA 18642
Made in: China
Value: $4.50 – 6.00
Description: Character is from the Nickelodeon TV show. Embossed on the back: "© 1993 NICKELODEON." Head only.

Dog Dish (Bingo)

Category: Miscellaneous
Contents: Colored candy pills
Size: 1⅛"h, 2⅛"w
Made for: The Topps Co., Duryea, PA 18642
Made in: China
Value: $3.00 – 4.00
Description: This dog dish is made in yellow, blue, red, and orange. It has different pictures of Bingo on the top. "Hollywood Hound, Life Guard, Party Dog, Bingo, Ruff Rider, and Cross-country Canine." Net Wt. 0.25 oz.

Donald Duck (Mickey's stuff)

Category: Gumball dispensers
Contents: Gumballs, 0.45 oz.
Size: 3½"h, 3"w, 2"d
Made for: Leaf Inc., Lake Forest, IL 60045
Made in: China
Cost new: $2.29 \ **Value:** $3.50 – 5.00
Description: ASI#4941628-A Comes on a card with a hole in it to operate. Donald is dressed as a fireman. Colored gumballs have Mickey's outline printed on them. Comes in a series of four. Mickey Mouse, Minnie Mouse, Goofy, and Donald Duck. © Disney.

Dot (Animaniacs)

Category: Characters
Contents: Gum, 0.4 oz.
Size: 2¾"h, 2"w, 1¾"d
Made for: Topps Co., Duryea, PA 18642
Made in: China
Value: $5.00 – 6.00
Description: From the Warner Brothers cartoon program, Animaniacs. Head only. Part of a series. © 1995. Embossed on the back: "™ & © Warner Bros."

Drum (Colonial)

Category: Miscellaneous
Contents: Candy, 1½ oz.
Size: 2⅛"h, 2"w
Made in: Hong Kong
Value: $10.00 – 14.00
Description: Paper label on the bottom reads "Colonial Drum With Candy." Comes with white with blue drumsticks.

Duck (Candy Pet)

Category: Animals
Contents: Colored candy beads
Size: 2⅞"h, 1¾"w, 1¾"d
Made for: Wizard Toys Inc., Bell, CA 90201
Made in: China
Value: $3.00 – 4.00
Description: There are six different Wizard Candy Pets: Bear, Cat, Chick, Dog, Duck, and Pig. They are sold on a card. Net Wt. 1 oz. The hat is the closure. Candy made in Canada. Item 7100.

Duck (Plucky)

Category: Animals
Contents: Sugarless candy, 0.2 oz.
Size: 2½"h, 1⅝"w, 1½"d
Made for: Topps Co., Duryea, PA 18642
Made in: China
Cost new: $0.99 \ **Value:** $4.00 – 6.00
Description: Plucky, a character from Warner Brothers', Tiny Toon Adventures. Head only. © 1991.

E.T. (full body)

Category: Characters
Contents: Colored candy pills, 0.4oz.
Size: 2¹³⁄₁₆"h (with head down), 1⅜"w, 1⅜"d
Made for: The Topps Co., Duryea, PA 18642
Made in: Hong Kong
Value: $5.00 – 6.00
Description: The extra-terrestrial container. Embossed on back: "© 1982 Universal Studios." E.T. has blue eyes and the neck extends.

E.T. (head and neck)

Category: Characters
Contents: Small colored pills, 0.4 oz.
Size: 2¾"h, 1¼"w, 1½"d
Made for: Topps Chewing Gum Inc., Duryea, PA 18642
Made in: Hong Kong
Value: $5.00 – 6.00
Description: The extra-terrestrial container. Embossed on back: "© Universal Studios." E.T. has blue eyes.

Earth Bank

Category: Miscellaneous
Contents: Gumballs, 3.5 oz.
Size: 5½"h, 3¹⁵⁄₁₆"w
Made for: Hilco Corp., Norristown, PA 19401
Made in: China
Cost new: $1.97 \ **Value:** $4.50 – 5.00
Description: This container came boxed. Globe spins on a stand. Can be refilled with candy and used as dispenser. Also has a slot for coin bank. Came in different colors. © 1997.

Egg (Christmas Bugs Bunny)

Category: Nonplastic
Contents: Foil-wrapped chocolate balls, 2 oz.
Size: 5⅛"h, 2⅞"w, 2½"d
Made for: Russell Stover Candies, Kansas City, MO 64106
Cost new: $2.49 \ **Value:** $3.00 – 4.00
Description: Christmas Bugs Bunny to double as tree ornament. Raised pictures on front and back. Container is made of tin, with string coming out of the top. © 1997.

Egg (Christmas Daffy Duck)

Category: Nonplastic
Contents: Foil-wrapped chocolate balls, 2 oz.
Size: 5⅛"h, 2⅞"w, 2½"d
Made for: Russell Stover Candies, Kansas City, MO 64106
Cost new: $2.49 \ **Value:** $3.00 – 4.00
Description: One of a series of Looney Tunes character Christmas ornaments. Daffy Duck appears on two sides. Tin egg-shaped container, © 1997.

Egg (Christmas Road Runner & Coyote with anvil)

Category: Nonplastic
Contents: Foil-wrapped chocolate balls, 2 oz.
Size: 5⅛"h, 2⅞"w, 2½"d
Made for: Russell Stover Candies, Kansas City, MO 64106
Cost new: $2.49 \ **Value:** $3.00 – 4.00
Description: Part of series of Christmas Looney Tunes ornaments. Featured: Road Runner and Wile E. Coyote. Container is made of tin, with hanging string. © 1997.

Egg (Christmas Road Runner & Coyote)

Category: Nonplastic
Contents: Foil-wrapped chocolate balls, 2 oz.
Size: 5⅛"h, 2⅞"w, 2½"d
Made for: Russell Stover Candies, Kansas City, MO 64106
Cost new: $2.49 \ **Value:** $3.00 – 4.00
Description: Road Runner and Wile E. Coyote are featured on this Christmas ornament, part of a Looney Tunes series. Tin container with string, © 1997.

Egg (Christmas Sylvester and Tweety)

Category: Nonplastic
Contents: Foil-wrapped chocolate balls, 2 oz.
Size: 5⅛"h, 2⅞"w, 2½"d
Made for: Russell Stover Candies, Kansas City, MO 64106
Cost new: $2.49 \ **Value:** $3.00 – 4.00
Description: Another in series of Looney Tunes Christmas ornaments. Featured: Sylvester and Tweety Bird. Front and back raised pictures. Containers made of tin, with string for hanging. © 1997.

Egg (Dove)

Category: Nonplastic
Contents: Milk chocolate eggs, 5 oz.
Size: 5⅛"h, 3¼"w, 3¼"d
Made for: M&M Mars Division of Mars, Inc., Hackettstown, NJ 07804-1503
Made in: China
Cost new: $4.49 \ **Value:** $4.50 – 5.50
Description: Made of tin. Dove Chocolate Promises™.

Egg (egg-sortment)

Category: Food items
Contents: Gum and candy, 8.43 oz.
Size: 6¼"h, 4⅞"w
Made for: Nabisco, Inc., East Hanover, NJ 07936
Cost new: $2.97 \ **Value:** $3.00 – 4.50
Description: Embossed on the bottom of the container: "© Planters Lifesavers Company." Has a dimple on top of the egg.

Egg (Hershey)

Category: Nonplastic
Contents: Chocolate kisses, 3 oz.
Size: 5⅛"h, 3¼"w
Made for: Hershey Chocolate U.S.A., Hershey, PA 17033-0815
Value: $2.00 – 2.50
Description: Has mama and baby bunny walking down a path carrying flowers. The container is made of paper and made in halves.

Egg (Jurassic Park)

Category: Food items
Contents: Candy, 0.4 oz.
Size: 2⅞"h, 2⅛"w
Made for: Topps Co., Duryea, PA 18642
Made in: China
Value: $3.00 – 4.50
Description: Picture of T. Rex and Jurassic Park, movie logo on front. Came with toy dinosaur and candy inside. On back side of label: "™ & © 1992 UNIVERSAL CITY STUDIOES, INC. & AMBLIN ENTERTAINMENT, INC."

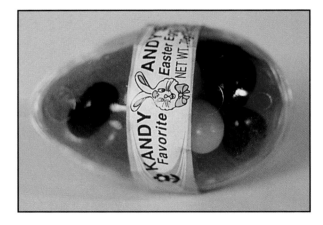

Egg (Kandy Andy's)

Category: Food items
Contents: Candy, 2.5 oz.
Size: 3⅜"h, 2³⁄₁₆"w, 2¼"d
Made for: E. Rosen Co., Pawtucket, RI 02860
Cost new: $0.99 \ **Value:** $1.00 – 1.50
Description: Paper label reads "Kandy Andy's Favorite Easter Egg." No markings on container.

Egg (M&M's)

Category: Food items
Contents: M&M's (plain), 2.0 oz
Size: 3¼"h, 2¼"w
Made for: Mars Inc., Hackettstown, NJ 07840-1503
Cost new: $0.49 \ **Value:** $1.00 – 1.50
Description: Plastic egg. Comes in different colors.

Egg (Mork)

Category: Food items
Contents: Bubble gum
Size: 2½"h, 1¾"w
Made for: Amurol Confections Co., Naperville, IL 60540
Value: $4.00 – 5.50
Description: Inside the egg are five seperately wrapped sticks of bubble gum with different sayings from Mork. It was made under license from Paramount Pictures Corp. The outside plastic reads "Mork Bubble Gum Net Wt. 0.52 oz."

Egg (See's)

Category: Nonplastic
Contents: See's candy
Size: 3⅝"h, 3¼"w, 5½"d
Made for: See's Candy Shop Inc., Los Angeles or San Fransico, CA
Made in: West Germany
Value: $3.00 – 5.00
Description: Printed inside is an Easter Bunny dancing with a ribbon that reads "See's Candies." Under the ribbon: "container made in Western Germany." Comes with Easter grass in plastic bag. Label on bag reads "Warning We recommend leaving Easter grass in bag. Grass can stick to candy and is not edible. Can be harmful if swallowed."

Egg (Werther's Easter)

Category: Food items
Contents: Werther's Original, 6 oz.
Size: 6¾"h, 3¾"w
Made for: Storck USA, Chicago, IL 60611
Made in: China
Cost new: $5.99 \ **Value:** $7.00 – 10.00
Description: Container comes in a box labeled:
"Werther's Original Easter Egg. © 1985."

Egg (wire)

Category: Food items
Contents: Candy, 1.4 oz.
Size: 3⅜"h, 2⅜"w, 2¼"d
Made for: Bee International, Chula Vista, CA 91914
Made in: China
Cost new: $1.00 \ **Value:** $1.50 – 2.00
Description: Plastic-coated wire arms and legs are
posable. Closure is a soft plastic push-in, on the back.
Top loop for string.

Egg Carton

Category: Food items
Contents: Bubble gum, 0.35 oz.
Size: ¾"h, 3⅛"w, 1¼"d
Made for: Topp Chewing Gum, Inc., Duryea, PA 18642
Made in: Hong Kong
Value: $5.00 – 6.00
Description: The sample on hand has the label damaged and can't read the full name. This is what
I can read "Y Farm Bubble Gum Net wt. 35 oz. made of dextrose, corn syrup, gum base, softeners,
artificial flavors. coloring, FD&C yellow no. 5 BHT (to maintain freshness). Distributed by © 1984
Topps Chewing Gum, Inc. Duryea, PA 18642. Made in Hong Kong #587."

Eggums

Category: Nonplastic
Contents: Gum, 0.8 oz.
Size: ¾"h, 3¾"w, 1½"d
Made for: Leaf Inc., Lake Forest, IL 60045
Made in: Canada
Cost new: $0.95 \ **Value:** $1.00 – 1.50
Description: Sold separately and in three-packs. Carton label
reads "Brightly Colored Bubble Gum Eggs." © 1993.

Elephant (sitting)

Category: Animals
Contents: Colored candy beads, ⅜ oz.
Size: 3⅛"h, 2³⁄₁₆"w, 1¾"d
Made for: E. Rosen Company, Pawtucket, RI
Made in: U.S.A.
Value: $7.00 – 8.50
Description: The only closure is the Scotch tape over the opening. #15 on back of the head. The label on the back has no zip code.

Fatso

Category: Characters
Contents: Gum
Size: 2⅛"h, 2¼"w, 1¹¹⁄₁₆"d
Made for: Topps Co., Duryea, PA 18642
Made in: China
Cost new: $1.29 \ **Value:** $3.00 – 4.00
Description: Featuring Fatso, one of Casper's friends. Glows in dark. Head only, with yellow eyes and black eyebrows. Embossed on the back: "Casper © 1995 UCS" and "AMBLIN ™Harvey."

Fire Engine 5

Category: Nonplastic
Contents: Assorted hard candy, 6 oz.
Size: 4"h, 3⅛"w, 7"d
Made for: Springwater Enterprises, Springboro, OH 45066
Made in: Mexico
Cost new: $3.97 \ **Value:** $5.00 – 6.00
Description: Container is made of tin. Wheels turn. Has "Engine 5" on the right side. Also has a coin slot on top. Purchased in 1997.

Fire Hydrant

Category: Miscellaneous
Contents: Colored candy shaped like dogs, 0.4 oz.
Size: 2¹³⁄₁₆"h, 1⁹⁄₁₆"w, 1½"d
Made for: Fleer Corp., Philadelphia, PA 19141
Value: $3.00 – 4.00
Description: Embossed on the bottom inside is #23, on the outside of the bottom is "Candy dextrose, citric acid, cal. stearate, art. flavor & color (FD & C yellow no. 5). Fleer Co. Phil. PA.19141 NET WT. .4 OZ."

Fish Box

Category: Miscellaneous
Contents: Colored pellets, 0.55 oz.
Size: ¾"h, 2⅜"w, 1⅞"d
Cost new: $0.49 \ **Value:** $1.00 – 1.50
Description: Has paper label with fish swimming with hearts, instead of bubbles. No markings on container.

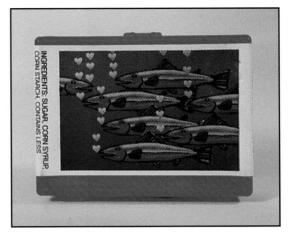

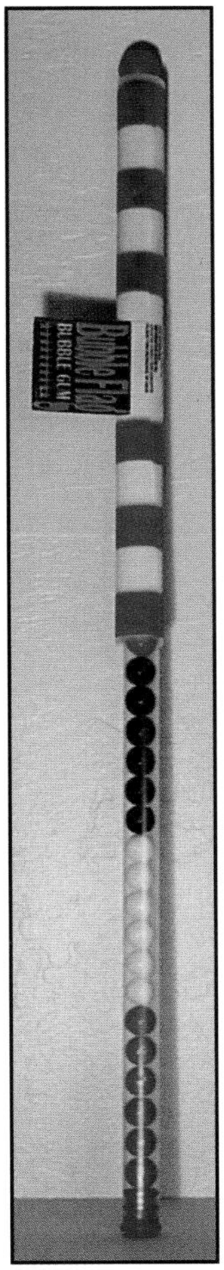

Flag (bubble)

Category: Miscellaneous
Contents: Gumballs, 2.5 oz.
Size: 24¾"h, 18¾"w, ⅞"d
Made for: Creative Confection Concepts, Milwaukee, WI 53209
Made in: U.S.A.
Cost new: $2.29 \ **Value:** $4.00 – 5.00
Description: Closure is push-in type. American flag made of plastic. Filled with red, white, and blue bubble gumballs. Printed on the flag: "Made in USA."

Flopits

Category: Miscellaneous
Contents: Small mint balls, 0.53 oz.
Size: 3¾"h, 3½"w, ⅜"d
Made for: Goodlite Products Inc., Bedford, TX 76021
Made in: China
Value: $4.00 – 5.00
Description: Container made to resemble a computer disk. Embossed on the back: "PATENT PENDING © JYCO 1995 CHINA."

Fly

Category: Animals
Contents: Gum, 0.3 oz.
Size: 1⅝"h, 2¾"w, 2¼"d
Made for: Topps Co., Duryea, PA 18642
Made in: China
Cost new: $0.49 \ **Value:** $3.50 – 4.00
Description: Has a suction cup on the bottom. Legs are soft rubber, body hard plastic. © 1992.

Flying Fist

Category: Games
Contents: Gumballs
Size: 6⁷⁄₁₆"h, 2⅛"w, 1¾"d
Made for: Creative Confection Concepts, Milwaukee, WI 93209
Made in: Mexico
Value: $3.50 – 4.00
Description: Clenched fist. Label reads "Flying Fist Fun Flying Toy! – Crunch Punch – All New Gum."

Flying Saucer (with alien)

Category: Battery operated
Contents: Colored candy beads
Size: 3⅜"h, 4"w
Made for: Bee International, Chula Vista, CA 91912
Made in: China
Cost new: $2.50 \ **Value:** $3.50 – 4.50
Description: If you push down on the Alien's head you dispense candy, the eyes light, and it makes a noise. It takes three AG13 batteries.

Flying Saucers

Category: Games
Contents: Tart 'n Tinys
Size: ⅝"h, 2½"w
Made for: Willy Wonka Candy Factory, Itasca, IL 60143
Value: $1.00 – 1.50
Description: Instructions on how to use it as a saucer are included. © The Willy Wonka Candy Factory.

Football (gum machine)

Category: Gum dispensers
Contents: Gum, 2.0 oz.
Size: 3⁷⁄₁₆"h, 3⅛"w, 2"d
Made for: Bee International, Chula Vista, CA 91912
Made in: China
Cost new: $0.99 \ **Value:** $2.00 – 3.00
Description: Embossed on the bottom: "© 1997 C. L. MADE IN CHINA." Embossed on the front are three bees. Turn the handle and the gum comes out. It is also made with a basketball, baseball, and soccerball.

Football (gumball machine)

Category: Gumball dispensers
Contents: Gumballs, 1.1 oz.
Size: 4¼"h, 4⁷⁄₁₆"w, 2¹¹⁄₁₆"d
Made for: Candy Containers & More Inc., Oxnard, CA 93030
Made in: China
Cost new: $0.95 \ **Value:** $2.00 – 3.00
Description: Comes in different colors. Turn handle on the front to get gumballs. Under paper label is embossed "PATENT PENDING MADE IN CHINA."

Fred Flintstone

Category: Characters
Contents: Pill-shaped with pictures of Flintstones characters, 0.3 oz.
Size: 2½"h, 1¹⁵⁄₁₆"w, 1⅜"d
Made for: Topps Co., Duryea, PA 18642
Made in: China
Cost new: $0.59 \ **Value:** $3.50 – 5.00
Description: It's Fred (the John Goodman version) from waist up. © 1993.

Freddy's

Category: Miscellaneous
Contents: Bubble gum, 0.4oz
Size: 3"h, 1¼"w, 1⅛"d
Made for: Topps Co., Duryea, PA 18642
Made in: Taiwan
Value: $3.00 – 4.00
Description: Comes with different pictures of Freddy on them. "™and © 1989-The Fourth New Line – Heron Venture. All rights reserved."

Frog

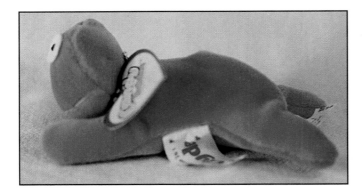

Category: Nonplastic
Contents: Colored candy pellets, 1.4oz.
Size: 2"h, 3"w, 5½"d
Made for: Cap Toys Inc., Bedford Hts., OH 44146
Made in: China
Cost new: $1.50 \ **Value:** $2.50 – 3.50
Description: This is one of the Candy Babies. It has candy in a plastic pack in its belly. Tag reads "My name is Clyde."

Front Loader

Category: Transportation
Contents: Colored candy beads
Size: 1⅞"h, 2"w, 2¾"d
Made in: Hong Kong
Value: $6.50 – 8.00
Description: The closure is a twist type located on the bottom. The loader and wheels of the container are movable. Embossed on the bottom is "Hong Kong." The front grill has six vertical lines. The side vents have three vertical liners on each side.

Frosty (ice cream cone)

Category: Food items
Contents: Candy pellets shaped as ice cream cones
Size: 3"h, 1⁵⁄₁₆"w
Value: $2.00 – 3.50
Description: Purchased in Yuma, Arizona, in 1996. Candy inside is shaped like tiny ice cream cones. There are no markings on the container. Probably made in Mexico.

Game Boy

Category: Miscellaneous
Contents: Gum, 1.05 oz.
Size: 4⁵⁄₁₆"h, 2½"w, ⅝"d
Made for: Amurol Products Co., Naperville, IL 60566
Made in: U.S.A.
Cost new: $0.99 \ **Value:** $2.00 – 3.00
Description: Container shaped like the Nintendo Game Boy™. Filled with bubblegum and trading cards. © 1993.

Garbage Can

Category: Miscellaneous
Contents: Candy, 0.4 oz.
Size: 2⅛"h, 1½"w
Made for: Topps Co., Duryea, PA 18642
Made in: China
Cost new: $0.49 \ **Value:** $2.00 – 3.00
Description: Although it is filled with candy, embossed on the bottom is "Topps Chewing Gum, Inc. © 1990."

Ghost (Slimer)

Category: Characters
Contents: Round, flat pressed candy with pictures on it, 0.4 oz.
Size: 2"h, 1⅝"w, 2"d
Made for: Topps Co., Duryea, PA 18642
Made in: China
Cost new: $0.49 \ **Value:** $3.50 – 5.00
Description: Slimer, of Ghostbusters fame. Embossed on the closure: "© 1989 Columbia Pictures Industries Inc. All rights reserved."

Giggle Gum

Category: Miscellaneous
Contents: Bubble gum, 3.17 oz.
Size: 6½"h, 1⅝"w
Made for: Amurol Confections Company, Yorkville, IL 60560
Made in: U.S.A.
Cost new: $1.95 \ **Value:** $2.50 – 3.50
Description: Makes Wacky sounds. It has a disk that slides back and forth when you shake it.

Glass (Hello Kitty)

Category: Miscellaneous
Contents: Candy balls, 0.17 oz.
Size: 2⅞"h, 1⅜"w
Made for: Sanrio, Inc., San Francisco, CA 94080
Made in: Japan
Cost new: $2.50 \ **Value:** $3.50 – 5.00
Description: "© 1976, 1997 Sanrio Co., LTD." It comes with candy inside the glass, and the closure is plastic whipped cream and fruit on top.

Glove and Ball (mini glove)

Category: Miscellaneous
Contents: Jelly beans
Size: 3⁷⁄₁₆"h, 3¼"w, 3¼"d
Made for: Treasure Chest Novelty Co., Walled Lake, MI
Made in: China
Cost new: $2.47 \ **Value:** $4.00 – 5.00
Description: Embossed on the bottom: "Treasure Chest Novelty Co. Made in China © /MLB 1996." The top of the baseball opens to get the candy.

Godzilla™ (Flix)

Category: Animals
Contents: Gumballs, 0.8 oz.
Size: 5⅝"h, 1⅝"w, 1⅝"d
Made for: Imagining 3
Made in: China
Value: $4.50 – 6.00
Description: Packaging label reads "Godzilla, King of the Monsters." It's a candy machine collectible. Embossed on the bottom: "Patents Pending Pats 5,385,267 D359, 232 made in China." © 1994.

Golf Club (Big Bubba)

Category: Games
Contents: Gum, 2.5 oz.
Size: 27¾"h, 3½"w, 2⅝"d
Made for: Creative Confection Concepts, Milwaukee, WI 53209
Made in: Mexico
Cost new: $2.99 \ **Value:** $5.00 – 6.00
Description: Comes with a ball. Filled with gumballs. Closer is screw-type on top of the club handle. It has "Big Bubba" embossed on the head of the club.

Golf Club (Ding)

Category: Games
Contents: Gum, 2.5 oz.
Size: 27"h, 4¼"w, 1⅛"d
Made for: Creative Confection Concepts, Milwaukee, WI 53209
Made in: Mexico
Cost new: $2.99 \ **Value:** $5.00 – 6.00
Description: Comes with a ball. Filled with gumballs. Closure is screw-type on top of club handle. Has "DING" and "Made in Mexico" embossed on head of the club.

Golf Club (Rattlers)

Category: Games
Contents: Gum, 2.5 oz.
Size: 26¾"h, 3⁵⁄₁₆"w, 1³⁄₁₆"d
Made for: Creative Confection Concepts, Milwaukee, WI 53209
Made in: Mexico
Cost new: $2.99 \ **Value:** $5.00 – 6.00
Description: Comes with a ball. Filled with gumballs. Closure is screw-type on top of the club's handle. It has "Rattler" embossed on back of the club head.

Gomez (Addams Family)

Category: Characters
Contents: Skull-and-bones-shaped candy, 0.28 oz.
Size: 4½"h, 2⅞"w, 1½"d
Made for: Bee International, Chula Vista, CA 91912
Made in: China
Value: $6.00 – 7.00
Description: Gomez from Addams Family movies. Embossed on the back: "© 1993 HBPC."

Goody Grabber

Category: Games
Contents: Gumballs, 0.2 oz.
Size: 3½"h, 3⁹⁄₁₆"w, 4⅞"d
Made for: Bee International, Chula Vista, CA 91912
Made in: China
Value: $4.50 – 6.00
Description: A crane type device. It has two controls to get the gumballs out. On the bottom are the operating instructions.

Goofy (Mickey's stuff)

Category: Characters
Contents: Gumballs, 0.45 oz.
Size: 3½"h, 3"w, 1⅝"d
Made for: Leaf Inc., Lake Forest, IL 60045
Made in: China
Cost new: $2.29 \ **Value:** $3.50 – 5.00
Description: ASI#4941627-A. Comes on a card with a hole in it to operate. Goofy is kneeling down sawing a board. Colored gumballs have Mickey's outline printed on them. Comes in a series of four: Mickey Mouse, Minnie Mouse, Goofy, and Donald Duck. © Disney.

Grapes

Category: Food items
Contents: Powdered candy, ⅝ oz.
Size: 2⅞"h, 1½"w
Made for: Ce De Candy Inc., Union, NJ 07083
Made in: U.S.A.
Cost new: $0.45 \ **Value:** $1.50 – 2.00
Description: Comes with a paper label under the screw cap. Cap has a ring for hanging as an ornament.

Grapes (Groovy)

Category: Food items
Contents: Bubble gum, 72g
Size: 4"h, 2⅜"w
Made for: Creative Confection Concepts, Milwaukee, WI 53209
Made in: Mexico
Cost new: $1.19 \ **Value:** $5.00 – 6.50
Description: Front of the tag reads "Groovy Grape, Gomme Balloune."

Gremlin

Category: Animals
Contents: Pressed candy in Gremlin shapes, 0.4 oz.
Size: 1¾"h, 2¾"w, 1⁷⁄₁₆"d
Made for: Topps Co., Duryea, PA
Made in: Hong Kong
Value: $8.00 – 9.00
Description: From the movie "Gremlins." Embossed on back of the neck: "© WB 1984." The later version has a green label with a bar code on it.

Gremlin #1

Category: Animals
Contents: Candy, 0.3 oz.
Size: 1⅞"h, 3³⁄₁₆"w, 1½"d
Made for: Topps Co., Duryea, PA 18642
Made in: China
Cost new: $0.49 \ **Value:** $4.50 – 6.50
Description: Another creature from "Gremlins." This one is cross-eyed. Made in 1990. Embossed on the bottom: "™ & © 1990 WARNER BROS., INC."

Gremlin #2

Category: Animals
Contents: Pressed candy shaped like Gremlins, 0.3 oz.
Size: 2¹⁄₁₆"h, 2⅞"w, 1⅝"d
Made for: Topps Co., Duryea, PA 18642
Made in: China
Cost new: $0.49 \ **Value:** $4.50 – 6.50
Description: From the Warner Brothers movie. Embossed on the bottom: "™ & © 1990 WARNER BROS., INC."

Gremlin #3

Category: Animals
Contents: Pressed candy shaped like Gremlins, 0.3 oz.
Size: 1⅞"h, 3⅛"w, 1⅝"d
Made for: Topps Co., Duryea, PA 18642
Made in: China
Cost new: $0.49 \ **Value:** $4.50 – 6.50
Description: Buck Tooth. Embossed on the bottom: "™ & © 1990 WARNER BROS., INC."

Gremlin #4

Category: Animals
Contents: Candy, 0.3 oz.
Size: 2"h, 2¹³⁄₁₆"w, 1½"d
Made for: The Topps Co. Inc., Duryea, PA 18642
Made in: China
Cost new: $0.49 \ **Value:** $4.50 – 6.50
Description: Red eyes, wrinkled neck, and comb on top of the head. Embossed on the bottom: "™ & © 1990 WARNER BROS., INC." Label is green with black writing.

Gremlin #5

Category: Animals
Contents: Candy, 0.4 oz
Size: 1¹⁵⁄₁₆"h, 2¹³⁄₁₆"w, 1⁷⁄₁₆"d
Made for: Topps Chewing Gum, Inc., Duryea, PA 18642
Made in: Hong Kong
Value: $8.00 – 9.00
Description: All green except for the eyes, and mouth which is red. Has big ears and a beard. Embossed on the back of the head: " © WB 1984."

Grimace (McDonald's)

Category: Characters
Contents: Nerds
Size: 2¾"h, 2¼"w, 1¾"d
Made for: McDonald's Corp., Oak Brook, IL 60521
Made in: China
Cost new: free w/Happy Meal \ **Value:** $1.00 – 2.00
Description: Marketed as McDonald's Happy Meal toy. One of a series of six. This one is number three. Plastic wrap has messages in English, French, and Spanish. It comes with a separate bag of Wonka Spooky Nerds candy. You can lift the mask on the container to see the character and put the candy in. The mask is the closure. Also there is a spring loaded door on the bottom. Embossed on the back of the container is "© 1998 McDonald's Corp. China/Chine TF 03."

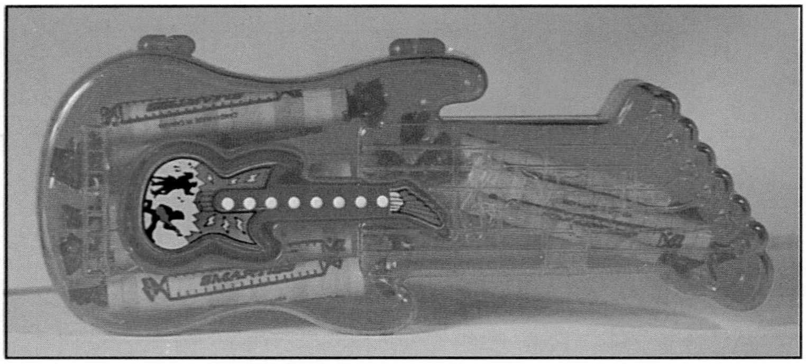

Guitar (eight tones)

Category: Battery operated
Contents: Smarties, 2$\frac{3}{8}$ oz.
Size: 3$\frac{5}{8}$"h, 8$\frac{5}{8}$"w, 1$\frac{1}{8}$"d
Made for: Hilco Corp., Norristown, PA 19401
Made in: Taiwan
Value: $4.50 – 6.00
Description: Battery operated, plays eight tones. Opens like a box and can be used to store small items. Has six strings; clef and four notes embossed on the front. Also embossed on the back, under the label: "made in Taiwan."

Guitar (round bottom)

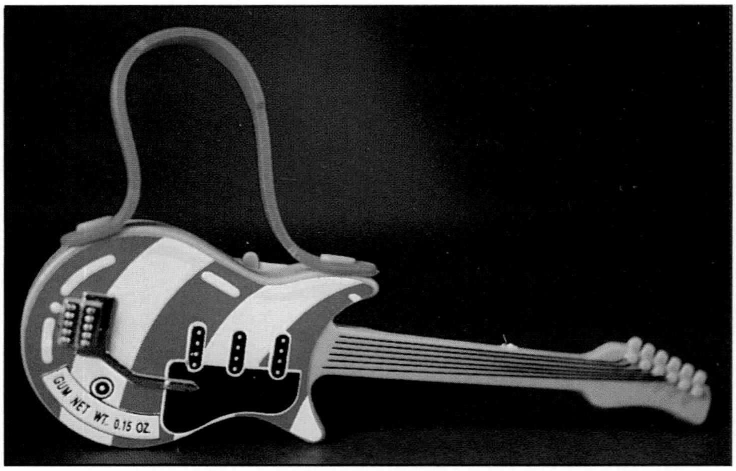

Category: Miscellaneous
Contents: Gum, 0.15 oz.
Size: 1$\frac{5}{8}$"h, 5"w, $\frac{11}{16}$"d
Made for: Topps Co., Duryea, PA 18642
Made in: China
Cost new: $0.50\ **Value:** $5.00 – 6.00
Description: Guitar came with a rubber strap. Push closure. © 1992.

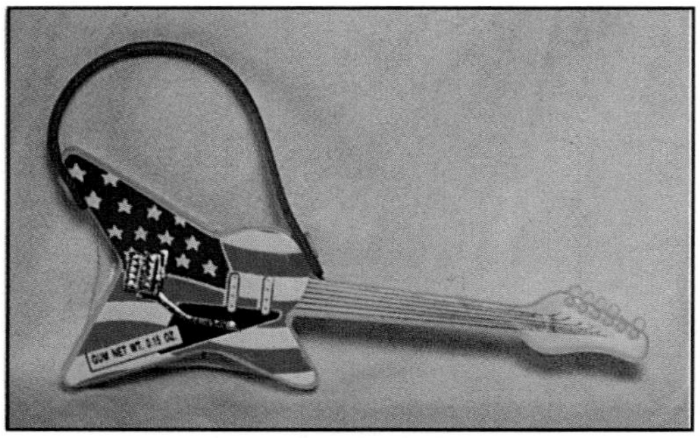

Guitar (v-shaped bottom)

Category: Miscellaneous
Contents: Gum, 0.15 oz.
Size: 2"h, 5$\frac{1}{16}$"w, $\frac{11}{16}$"d
Made for: Topps Co., Duryea, PA 18642
Made in: China
Cost new: $0.50\ **Value:** $5.00 – 6.00
Description: Came with a rubber strap. Push closure. © 1992.

Gumball Machine (candy shop)

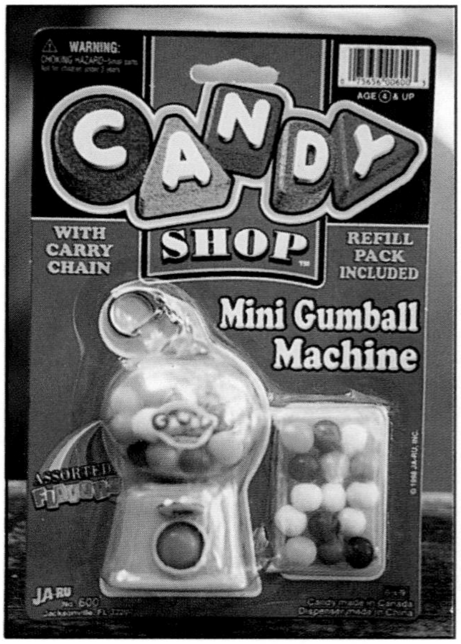

Category: Gumball dispensers
Contents: Gumballs
Size: 3$\frac{7}{8}$"h, 2$\frac{1}{4}$"w, 1$\frac{5}{8}$"d
Made for: JA-RU, INC. Jacksonville, FL 32207
Made in: China
Value: $2.00 – 3.00
Description: Comes on a card marked "Candy Shop with carry chain – refill pack included. Mini Gumball Machine. © 1998 JA-RU, INC. No. 600."

Gumball Machine (Fleer)

Category: Gumball dispensers
Contents: Candy, 0.4 oz.
Size: 2¼"h, 1½"w, 1½"d
Made for: Fleer Co., Philadelphia, PA 19141
Cost new: $0.49 \ **Value:** $2.00 – 3.00
Description: Has a flat top that is embossed with "Sugar dextrose, starch, artificial flavor & color, FD&C yellow no. 5. carnauba wax. Dist. by Fleer Co. Phila. Pa. 19141 NET WT. 0.4 oz." Embossed on the door is the word "Candy."

Gumball Machine (Garfield)

Category: Gumball dispensers
Contents: Gumballs, 3oz.
Size: 9½"h, 3"w, 3⅜"d
Made for: Bee International, Chula Vista, CA 91912
Made in: China
Cost new: $2.50 \ **Value:** $4.00 – 6.00
Description: This is also a bank. Garfield is made out of rubber. The container is plastic. Embossed on the bottom is "© 1998 U.C.L. MADE IN CHINA OPEN<———> CLOSE." Comes in a three-sided box labeled "Gumball Machine – Coin Bank – with collectable toy topper!"

Gumball Machine (Hulk)

Category: Gumball dispensers
Contents: Gum, 0.8 oz.
Size: 5⅝"h, 1¾"w, 1¼"d
Made for: Imaginings 3, Niles, IL 60714
Made in: China
Cost new: $1.57 \ **Value:** $3.50 – 5.50
Description: ™ & © 1996 Marvel Characters, Inc. Marvel Supper Heroes. Collectible Gumball Machine. Flix, For ages 3 and up. Embossed on the bottom: "Patent Pending Pats 5,385,287-D359, 232 Made in China."

Gumball Machine (Sweet & Fun)

Category: Gumball dispensers
Contents: Colored candy balls, 1.23oz.
Size: 4"h, 2³⁄₁₆"w, 2½"d
Made for: Sunco Ltd.
Made in: China
Cost new: $0.99 \ **Value:** $2.00 – 2.50
Description: It has a lever on the side to slide forward and get the candy out. The label on the bottom reads "All rights reserved. Sweet & Fun is a trademark of Sunco Ltd. PNo. 7468828 Int'l Patent Pending. © 1997 Sunco Ltd. Item No. 9012." Candy made in Canada. Packaged in Canada. Embossed on the bottom: "© 1997 Sunco P NO. 7468828 – MADE IN CHINA."

Gumball Machine (Wolverine)

Category: Gumball dispensers
Contents: Gumballs, 0.8 oz.
Size: 6"h, 1⅝"w, 1⅜"d
Made for: Imaginings 3, Niles, IL 60714
Made in: China
Cost new: $1.57 \ **Value:** $3.50 – 5.50
Description: ™ & © 1996 Marvel Characters, Inc. Flix, For ages 3 and up. Marvel Super Heroes. Collectible Gumball Machine. Comes with ten extra gumballs.

Gumball Machine Tall (Hulk)

Category: Gumball dispensers
Contents: Gumballs, 1.5 oz.
Size: 12"h, 2"w, 1⁷⁄₁₆"d
Made for: Imagining 3, Niles, IL 60714
Made in: China
Cost new: $2.24 \ **Value:** $3.50 – 4.50
Description: Paper packaging reads "Flix, Marvel Super Heroes, Collectible Gumball Machine, For ages 3 and up." Pat. 5,385,267 – D359, 232. © 1996.

Gumball Machine Tall (Spider-Man)

Category: Gumball dispensers
Contents: Gumballs, 1.5 oz.
Size: 12"h, 2"w, 1⅜"d
Made for: Imagining 3, Niles, IL 60714
Made in: China
Cost new: $2.24 \ **Value:** $3.50 – 4.50
Description: Gumball machine featuring Spider-Man. © 1996. Paper packaging reads "Flix, Marvel Super Heroes, Collectible Gumball Machine, For ages 3 and up." Pat. 5,385,267 – D359, 232. © 1996.

Gumball Machine Tall (Wolverine)

Category: Gumball dispensers
Contents: Gumballs, 1.5 oz.
Size: 12¼"h, 2"w, 1⅜"d
Made for: Imagining 3, Niles, IL 60714
Made in: China
Cost new: $2.24 \ **Value:** $3.50 – 4.50
Description: Featuring Wolverine of the X-Men. Paper packaging reads "Flix, Marvel Super Heroes, Marvel Comics™, Collectible Gumball Machine." Pat. 5,385,267 – D359, 232. © 1996.

Gumball Wizard

Category: Gumball dispensers
Contents: Colored candy beads, 1 oz.
Size: 4⅛"h, 1⅞"w
Made for: Wizard Toys, Inc., Mesa, AZ 85204
Made in: China
Cost new: $2.16 \ **Value:** $2.00 – 3.00
Description: Comes on a card. Item #6020. The back of the card reads "Original pocket size micro wizard. Fits easily in your pocket or purse." Dispenses tiny candy treats. Available in four colors – red, yellow, blue, and purple.

Gun (E. Rosen)

Category: Miscellaneous
Contents: Colored candy beads, ⅜ oz.
Size: 2⁹⁄₁₆"h, 1"w, 5¼"d
Made for: E. Rosen Company, Pawtucket, RI 02860
Made in: U.S.A.
Value: $7.00 – 8.50
Description: Embossed on the left side of the grip is a picture of a cowboy and "NESW," on the right side, a cowboy only. The barrel and body are engraved. There is no closure. Tape over the end of the barrel keeps the candy in. Compare this with Gun (N-E-S-W.)

Gun (Laser)

Category: Miscellaneous
Contents: Candy balls
Size: 4⅛"h, 6⅜"w, ⁷⁄₁₆"d
Made in: China
Cost new: $1.49 \ **Value:** $3.00 – 4.00
Descripton: The label on the gun reads "Laser Candy Gun. Not suitable for children under 3 years old because of small parts. Keep in cool area (under 13 c). Don't shoot to humans."

Gun (N-E-S-W)

Category: Miscellaneous
Contents: Colored candy beads
Size: 2⁷⁄₁₆"h, 1"w, 5"d
Made for: Allen Mitchell Products, Oxnard, CA 93030
Made in: Hong Kong
Cost new: $0.59 \ **Value:** $4.00 – 7.00
Description: Embossed on left side of the grip is picture of cowboy and "NESW." On the right side, a cowboy only. Closure is push-in under handle.

Gun (X-Men)

Category: Battery operated
Contents: Gum, 0.9 oz.
Size: 4⅛"h, 4¾"w, 1"d
Made for: Classic Heroes Inc., Stuart, FL 34995
Made in: China
Value: $4.50 – 6.00
Description: Plastic laser gun features the X-Men. Battery-operated sound effects. Embossed on left side of the grip: "© 1995 Classic Heroes, Inc. made in China."

Gun (water pistol)

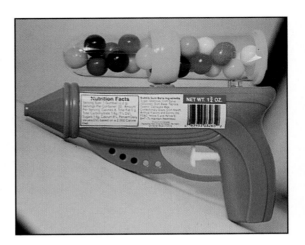

Category: Miscellaneous
Contents: Gumballs, 1¾ oz.
Size: 5⅝"h, 1⅝"w, 7"d
Made for: Hilco Corp., Norristown, PA 19401
Made in: China
Cost new: $1.97 \ **Value:** $2.50 – 3.50
Description: Looks like a water pistol with gumballs in upper cylinder. Embossed on left side: "HILCO corporation Made in China."

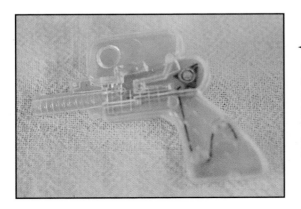

Gun with Crank

Category: Miscellaneous
Contents: Small colored candy beads
Size: 2"h, 2⅞"w, ¹³⁄₁₆"d closure to crank
Made in: Hong Kong
Value: $8.00 – 10.00
Description: Comes in different colors. It will shoot out candy! Turn the crank and candy comes out the barrel of the gun.

Hamburglar® (McDonald's)

Category: Characters
Contents: Nerds
Size: 2⅞"h, 2"w, 1⅝"d
Made for: McDonald's Corp., Oak Brook, IL 60521
Made in: China
Cost new: free w/Happy Meal \ **Value:** $1.00 – 2.00
Description: Marketed as McDonald's Happy Meal toy. One of a series of 6. This one is #6. Plastic wrap has messages in English, French, and Spanish. It comes with a separate bag of Wonka Spooky Nerds candy. You can lift the mask on the container to see the character and put the candy in. The mask is the closure. Also there is a spring loaded door on the bottom. Embossed on the bottom of the container is "© 1998 McDonald's Corp. China KH Chine."

Harry (and the Hendersons)

Category: Characters
Contents: Candy, 0.4 oz.
Size: 2⅜"h, 1⅝"w, 1⁷⁄₁₆"d
Made for: Topps Chewing Gum Inc., Duryea, PA 18642
Made in: Hong Kong
Value: $5.50 – 7.50
Description: The Bigfoot creature from the movie "Harry and the Hendersons." Embossed on the bottom: "HARRY AND THE HENDERSONS™ © 1987 UNIV. STUDIOS."

Heart

Category: Miscellaneous
Contents: Hearts, 0.35 oz.
Size: 2½"h, 2⁹⁄₁₆"w, 1⁷⁄₁₆"d
Made for: Bee International, Chula Vista, CA 91912
Made in: China
Cost new: $0.59 \ **Value:** $1.00 – 1.50
Description: Transparent heart with heart-shaped candy inside. Carrying cord attached. Comes in a plastic bag decorated with blue hearts.

Heart (Be My Valentine)

Category: Holiday
Contents: Cinnamon hearts, 1.5 oz.
Size: 3"h, 2¾"w, ⅞"d
Made for: E. Rosen Co., Pawtucket, RI 02860
Cost new: $0.69 \ **Value:** $1.50 – 2.00
Description: Paper label reads "Be My Valentine – Cinnamon Hearts."

Heart (Hallmark)

Category: Miscellaneous
Contents: Candy
Size: 5¼"h, 5¾"w, 1⅝"d
Made for: Hallmark Cards Inc.
Cost new: $3.25 \ **Value:** $6.00 – 7.00
Description: This container is see-through red plastic with white printing which reads "SWEET TREATS." The opening is on the bottom side of the container.

Heart (Hugs & Kisses)

Category: Miscellaneous
Contents: Hugs & Kisses, 6 oz.
Size: Boxed 6⅜"h, 4¹⁵⁄₁₆"w, 3⅛"d
Made for: Hershey Chocolate U.S.A., Hershey, PA 17033-0815
Made in: U.S.A.
Value: $3.00 – 4.50
Description: Heart-shaped container is also a candy dish. © 1994 Hershey Corp. There are no markings on the container.

Heart (Kiss Me)

Category: Miscellaneous
Contents: Runts® mini-hearts, 7 oz.
Size: 4"h, 3⅞"w, 2¼"d
Made for: The Jelly Bean Factory, Fairfax, OH 45227
Made in: China
Cost new: $2.47 \ **Value:** $2.50 – 3.50
Description: Made in two pieces. Embossed on tab (top) is "GW" on one side and "China" on the other. The words "Kiss Me" are painted on the front in white.

Heart (M&M's)

Category: Miscellaneous
Contents: M&M plain
Size: 3⅜"h, 3½"w, 2⅜"d
Made for: M&M Mars Division of Mars, Inc., Hackettstown, NJ 07804-1503
Made in: China
Cost new: $1.29 \ **Value:** $2.00 – 3.00
Description: Covered with a clear plastic wrap with a picture of Red M&M on it. Embossed on the front of the container is Red M&M with his right hand raised and left hand on his hip. Or where his hip should be.

Heart (Space Jam)

Category: Miscellaneous
Contents: Cotton candy powder, 1.5 oz.
Size: 3⁵⁄₁₆"h, 2¾"w, 1¼"d
Made for: Creative Confection Concepts, Milwaukee, WI 53209
Made in: Mexico
Cost new: $1.00 \ **Value:** $4.00 – 5.00
Description: From the Warner Brothers movie starring Bugs Bunny and Michael Jordan. Container features Bugs with heart coming out of his chest on one side. The other side features Lola Bunny. Comes with plastic string. © 1996.

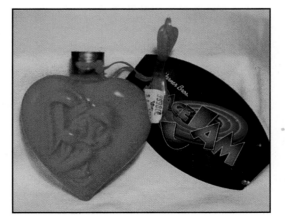

Heart (Tuntoys)

Category: Miscellaneous
Contents: Gum
Size: 2"h, 1¹⁵⁄₁₆"w, ¾"d
Made for: Tuntoys
Made in: Mexico
Cost new: $0.25 \ **Value:** $1.00 – 1.50
Description: Purchased container in Yuma, Arizona, in 1996. Label reads "Dulces/TUNTOYS/Jugueres." Container has Cupid on both sides. Closure is push-in with a cord in it.

Heart (wire)

Category: Miscellaneous
Contents: Pressed heart shapes, 0.5 oz.
Size: 2½"h, 3³⁄₁₆"w, 1¾"d (heart only)
Made in: China
Cost new: $0.99 \ **Value:** $2.00 – 3.00
Description: Container doubles as an ornament with string through ring on top of the heart. Arms and legs are plastic-covered wire so they can be repositioned.

Helicopter (green)

Category: Transportation
Contents: Small colored candy balls
Size: 1½"h, ⅝"w, 3"d
Made in: Hong Kong
Value: $4.00 – 6.00
Description: Shaped like an army transport helicopter with two propellers. Embossed underneath main prop: "Made in Hong Kong." Small plastic bag of candy inside.

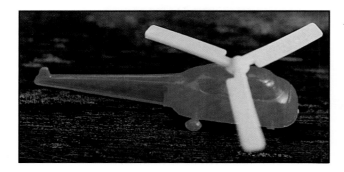

Helicopter (pink)

Category: Transportation
Contents: Small colored candy balls
Size: ¾"h, ¾"w, 2⁹⁄₁₆"d
Made in: West Germany
Value: $4.00 – 6.00
Description: Has three-blade, moveable propeller with "W-Germany" embossed on one blade. Paper closure on the bottom.

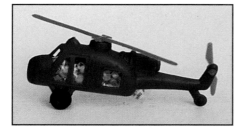

Helicopter (three-wheel)

Category: Transportation
Contents: Small colored candy balls
Size: 11⅛"h, ⅝"w, 3"d
Made for: Bee, Los Angeles, CA
Made in: Hong Kong
Value: $4.00 – 6.00
Description: Has three openings on each side, plus two in front. "Made in Hong Kong" embossed under the main prop. Bag of candy inside.

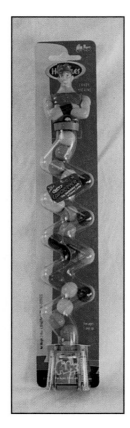

Hercules (candy machine)

Category: Characters
Contents: Gobstoppers, 2.48 oz.
Size: 12⅛"h, 2"w, 1⅜"d
Made for: Imagining 3, Niles, IL 60714
Made in: China
Cost new: $2.24 \ **Value:** $3.50 – 4.50
Description: From Disney's "Hercules." Label reads "Flix, Disney's Hercules, Candy Machine. For ages 3 and up." Pat. 5,385,267-D359,232.

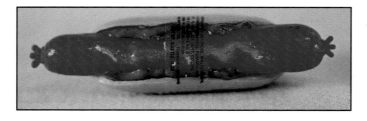

Hot Dog

Category: Food items
Contents: Candy
Size: 1⅝"h, 4½"w, 1¼"d
Made for: Bee International, Commerce, CA 90040
Made in: Hong Kong
Value: $12.00 – 15.00
Description: Embossed on the side is "© B.I. 1985." The hot dog has relish on each side and mustard in the middle.

Hot Wheels

Category: Miscellaneous
Contents: Sours candy, 1 oz.
Size: ⅞"h, 2½"w
Made for: BerZerk Candy Werks, Memphis, TN 38119
Cost new: $0.50 \ **Value:** $1.00 – 2.00
Description: Inside container: wheel-shaped candy. Licensed by Mattel. © 1992.

Iam Hungry™ *(McDonald's)*

Category: Characters
Contents: Nerds
Size: 2½"h, 2"w, 2⅛"d
Made for: McDonald's Corp., Oak Brook, IL 60521
Made in: China
Cost new: free w/Happy Meal \ **Value:** $1.00 – 2.00
Description: Marketed as McDonald's Happy Meal toy. One of a series of six. This is number one. Plastic wrap has messages in English, French, and Spanish. It comes with a separate bag of Wonka Spooky Nerds candy. You can lift the mask on the container to see the character and put the candy in. The mask is the closure. Also there is a spring loaded door on the bottom. Embossed on the bottom of the container is "© 1998 McDonald's Corp. China WM Chine."

Ice (Blitz)

Category: Miscellaneous
Contents: Power mints
Size: 2¾"h, 1¾"w, ⅝"d
Made for: Schuster Marketing Corp., Milwaukee, WI 53220
Made in: Great Britain
Cost new: $1.99 \ **Value:** $2.00 – 3.00
Description: Made to look like a cigarette lighter. Embossed on the bottom: "Blitz Design Corp. Pat. Pend." A number "5" inside the recycle symbol and "PP" under it.

Ice Cream Cone

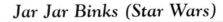

Category: Food items
Contents: Colored candy in ice cream cone and sundae shapes, 0.4 oz.
Size: 2¼"h, 1½"w
Made for: Topps Co., Duryea, PA 18642
Made in: China
Cost new: $0.49 \ **Value:** $3.50 – 5.00
Description: © 1990.

Jar Jar Binks (Star Wars)

Category: Transportation
Contents: Tart 'n Tinys, 1.58 oz.
Size: 4⅝"h, 2⅜"w
Made for: Cap Candy
Made in: China
Cost new: $2.97 \ **Value:** $3.00 – 4.00
Description: Some kind of space craft. On top is a raised picture of Jar Jar Binks. When you remove the closer a control panel is visible. Inside is a package of candy in a plastic bag. The outside label reads "STAR WARS EPISODE 1 Jar Jar Binks Film Action Container. Cap Candy item NO. 4687 © Lucasfilm Ltd. & ™ © 99 OddzOn, Inc. A subsidiary of Hasbro, Inc. Napa, CA 94558. All rights reserved. Made in China. Wonka™ and Tarts n Tiny's are trademarks of NESTLE USA, INC. Confection Division, Itasca, IL 60143 USA."

Jessie (Toy Story 2)

Category: Characters
Contents: Candy
Size: 7¹⁄₁₆"h, 2³⁄₁₆"w, 2"d
Made for: McDonald's Corp., Oak Brook, IL 60521
Made in: China
Cost new: $2.50 \ **Value:** $3.00 – 5.00
Description: This candy-filled toy is also a kaleidoscope. It has a hole in her hat to look through. Embossed on the bottom is "Mfg. for McD Corp. China/Chine SV 10 © 1999 McDonald's Corp. © Disney/Pixar." Mini Chewy Spree candy, Net Wt. 1.20 oz. One in a series of six.

Joker

Category: Characters
Contents: Pill-shaped candy
Size: 2³⁄₈"h, 1¼"w, 1½"d
Made for: The Topps Co., Duryea, PA 18642
Made in: Hong Kong
Value: $6.00 – 7.50
Description: Embossed on the bottom: "© DC Comics Inc. 1989." The candy has a bat on one side and the word "Batman" on the other. Net Wt. 0.3 oz.

Jump Rope

Category: Games
Contents: Fruit-shaped Runts
Size: 5½"h, 1¼"w
Made for: Imperial Toy Corporation 1996, Los Angeles, CA 90021
Made in: China
Cost new: $2.29 \ **Value:** $2.29 – 3.50
Description: To get candy, twist the handle off of the cap. Filled with Willy Wonka's fruit-shaped Runts. Candy Club.

Jump Shot

Category: Games
Contents: Gumballs, 0.2 oz.
Size: 3¾"h, 2¾"w, 3³⁄₈"d
Made for: Bee International, Chula Vista, CA 91912
Made in: China
Value: $5.00 – 6.50
Description: To get the gumballs out, you make a basket by pushing down the lever in front and let it go. Fun toy.

Junior (Jungle Book)

Category: Characters
Contents: Nerds
Size: 2⁷⁄₁₆"h, 2⁵⁄₁₆"w, 3⅛"d
Made for: McDonald's Corp., Oak Brook, IL 60251
Made in: China
Cost new: free w/Happy Meal \ **Value:** $2.00 – 4.00
Description: McDonald's Happy Meal toy. One from a series of Disney's Jungle Book. Embossed on the right hind leg: "MFG. FOR McDCORP © DISNEY CHINA/CHINE WI 23."

Kaa (Jungle Book)

Category: Characters
Contents: Nerds
Size: 4⅜"h, 2⅞"w
Made for: McDonald's Corp., Oak Brook, IL 60521
Made in: China
Cost new: free w/Happy Meal \ **Value:** $2.00 – 4.00
Description: McDonald's Happy Meal toy. One from a series of Disney's Jungle Book. Embossed on the bottom: "MFG. FOR McD CORP CHINA KH CHINE © DISNEY."

Keepsake Box

Category: Nonplastic
Contents: Cherry hard candy
Size: 1¾"h, 3¾"w, 2⅞"d
Made for: The Jelly Bean Factory, Fairfax, OH 45227
Made in: China
Cost new: $2.97 \ **Value:** $3.00 – 4.00
Description: Container is made out of paper and cloth with sequence on top. © GAC.

Keyboard (Candy Keyboard)

Category: Battery operated
Contents: Smarties, 2.5 oz.
Size: 1⁵⁄₁₆"h, 7¹³⁄₁₆"w, 2½"d
Made for: BerZerk Candy Werks, Memphis, TN 38119
Made in: China
Value: $4.50 – 6.00
Description: Container-keyboard has 13 buttons to push. Came with eight rolls of Smarties inside and song book. Book gives directions for six songs. © 1994.

King Louie (Jungle Book)

Category: Characters
Contents: Nerds
Size: 3"h, 2⅝"w, 2"d
Made for: McDonald's Corp., Oak Brook, IL 60521
Made in: China
Cost new: free w\Happy Meal\ **Value:** $2.00 – 4.00
Description: Came with McDonald's Happy Meal. One from a series from Disney's Jungle Book characters. Embossed on the bottom: "MFG. FOR McD CORP. CHINA SW CHINE © DISNEY."

Kryptonite

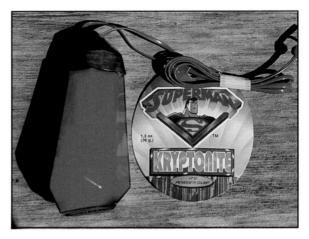

Category: Miscellaneous
Contents: Gum, 1.3 oz.
Size: 3⅝"h, 1⅝"w
Made for: Creative Confection Concepts, Milwaukee, WI 53209
Made in: Mexico
Cost new: $1.19 \ **Value:** $4.00 – 6.50
Description: Has a plastic cord. Label reads: "Superman Kryptonite, it's power gum!" Screw-on closure. Embossed on the side: "made in Mexico, ™ & © 1997 DC Comics."

Label Machine

Category: Miscellaneous
Contents: Bubble gum, 1.23 oz.
Size: 2¹⁵⁄₁₆"h, 2½"w, 4¼"d
Made for: Au'some Candies Inc., Westlake Village, CA 91361
Made in: China
Cost new: $1.99 \ **Value:** $3.50 – 4.00
Description: This is made like a label machine. You can spell out anything you want. It only has letters, A – Z, no numbers. On top is written, "Print your own secret message™."

Laguna Lime

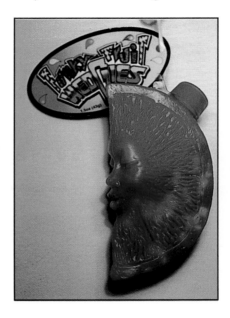

Category: Food items
Contents: Bubble gum, 1.5 oz.
Size: 4⅜"h, 2⅜"w, 1½"d
Made for: Creative Confection Concepts, Milwaukee, WI 53209
Made in: Mexico
Cost new: $1.19 \ **Value:** $4.00 – 6.50
Description: Label tied with plastic cord that reads "Funky Fruit Wedgies." Part of a series of four: Laguna Lime, Kiwi Strawberry, Luscious Lemon, and Maui Orange.

Lamp (hurricane)

Category: Miscellaneous
Contents: Colored candy beads, ¼ oz.
Size: 4¼"h, 2³⁄₁₆"w, 1¾"d
Made for: E. Rosen Company, Pawtucket, RI 02860
Made in: Hong Kong
Value: $9.00 – 12.00
Description: Embossed on the bottom: "MADE IN HONG KONG." The closure is ⅞"h x ⅝"w. Push in type.

Light Globe

Category: Miscellaneous
Contents: Gum
Size: 2⅞"h, 1⅝"w
Cost new: $0.25 \ **Value:** $1.50 – 2.50
Description: No markings and no label. Purchased in Yuma, Arizona, in 1996 from a Mexican vendor at a flea market. Has plastic string to be worn around the neck.

Link

Category: Characters
Contents: Gum, 0.8 oz.
Size: 3⅜"h, 1¹⁵⁄₁₆"w, 1¼"d
Made for: Topps Co., Duryea, PA 18642
Made in: Taiwan
Value: $3.50 – 6.50
Description: Featuring the video game character. Came in many colors. Embossed on the bottom: "© 1989 NOA."

Lipstick

Category: Miscellaneous
Contents: Pressed candy shaped like lipstick
Size: 1¹³⁄₁₆"h, ⅝"w
Made in: China
Cost new: $0.25 \ **Value:** $0.50 – 1.00
Description: Definitely aimed at girls. Candy inside is also lipstick-shaped. Embossed on the side: "For EC countries," followed by long list of ingredients.

Little House of Horrors

Category: Miscellaneous
Contents: Colored candy pill shape, 0.04 oz.
Size: 2⅜"h, 1⁷⁄₁₆"w, 1⅞"d
Made for: Topps Co., Duryea, PA 18642
Made in: Hong Kong
Value: $6.00 – 7.50
Description: Embossed on the base of the plant, "© 1986 The Geffen Film Company." Under the base is the letter "K." On the inside of the flowerpot is the letter "N". Green tape is wrapped around the mouth of the plant to make it tamper-proof.

Little Mermaid (Flix)

Category: Gumball dispensers
Contents: Gumballs, 0.54 oz.
Size: 5¾"h, 1¹¹⁄₁₆"w, 1⅜"d
Made for: Imagining 3, Niles, IL 60714
Made in: China
Cost new: $2.75 \ **Value:** $4.00 – 5.00
Description: Gumball machine. Has "Flix" embossed on the front, and "patents pending – 5,385,267, D358, 232 Made in China," on the bottom.

Locomotive

Category: Transportation
Contents: Gum, 3 oz.
Size: 3¾"h, 2¾"w, 5⅛"d
Made for: Bee International, Chula Vista, CA 91912
Made in: China
Cost new: $2.99 \ **Value:** $4.00 – 5.00
Description: Has coin slot to be used as a bank. Four wheels, all turn. Embossed on the bottom: "Made in China."

Locomotive (big stack)

Category: Transportation
Contents: Colored candy beads
Size: 2⅜"h, 1¼"w, 3¾"d
Made for: E. Rosen Co., Pawtucket, NJ 02820
Value: $25.00 – 30.00
Description: This engine has two wheels on each side. The front wheel has eight indentations on it and the rear wheel only has five indentations. It has a loop to insert a string on the front.

Lunch Box (Betty Boop)

Category: Nonplastic
Contents: Candy, 3.8 oz.
Size: 4¹³⁄₁₆"h, 5⅝"w, 2⅜"d
Made for: American Specialty Confections, Inc., Lancaster, PA 17603
Made in: China
Cost new: $8.95 \ **Value:** $9.00 – 12.00
Description: Printed on the bottom of the box: "© 1997 King Features Syndicate, Inc./Fleischer Studios, Inc. ™The Hearst Corporation. #13." The label on the back reads "This limited edition collector's tin may contain one or more of the following nostalgic candies: Butterscotch Buttons, Dubble Bubble®, Jolly Rancher®, Lemonheads®, Mary Janes®, Smarties®, Starlight Mints, or Tootsie Roll®. Net Wt. 3.8 oz."

Lunch Box (Curious George)

Category: Nonplastic
Contents: Candy, 3.8 oz
Size: 4¹³⁄₁₆"h, 5⅝"w, 2⅜"d
Made for: American Specialty Confections, Inc., Lancaster, PA 17603
Made in: China
Cost new: $8.95 \ **Value:** $9.00 – 12.00
Description: Has pictures of George doing different things on the side and bottom of the container. Printed on the bottom of the box: "#21 Curious George®, created by Margaret and H.A. Rey, is copyrighted and trademarked by Mifflin Co. and used under license by Universal Studio." The label on the back reads "This limited edition collector's tin may contain one or more of the following nostalgic candies: Butterscotch Buttons, Dubble Bubble®, Jolly Rancher®, Lemonheads®, Mary Janes®, Smarties®, Starlight Mints, or Tootsie Roll®. Net Wt. 3.8 oz."

Lunch Box (Kiss for You)

Category: Nonplastic
Contents: Hershey's Kisses, 10 oz.
Size: 6½"h, 7¾"w, 2⅞"d
Made for: Hershey Chocolate U.S.A., Hershey, PA 17033-0815
Made in: U.S.A.
Value: $9.00 – 10.00
Description: Made of tin with a plastic handle filled with chocolate candy kisses. Has pictures of kisses on the sides, top and bottom. Sealed with plastic wrap with a paper label on the bottom.

Lunch Box (Nancy & Sluggo)

Category: Nonplastic
Contents: Candy, 3.8 oz.
Size: 4¹³⁄₁₆"h, 5⅝"w, 2³⁄₁₆"d
Made for: American Specialty Confections, Inc., Lancaster, PA 17603
Made in: China
Cost new: $8.95 \ **Value:** $9.00 – 12.00
Description: This lunch box has Nancy & Sluggo cartoons on the sides and bottom. Printed on the bottom in white letters: "Nancy™ & Sluggo™ © United Feature Sydicate, Inc. A.S.C. Lancaster, PA 17603 #18." There is no "n" in syndicate. The label on the back reads "This limited edition collector's tin may contain one or more of the following nostalgic candies: Butterscotch Buttons, Dubble Bubble®, Jolly Rancher®, Lemonheads®, Mary Janes®, Smarties®, Starlight Mints, or Tootsie Roll®. 3.8 oz."

Lunch Box (Reese's)

Category: Nonplastic
Contents: Milk chocolate peanut butter cups, 8 oz.
Size: 6⅛"h, 7¾"w, 2¹⁵⁄₁₆"d
Made for: H.B. Reese Candy Co. (Hershey Foods), Hershey, PA 17011-0815
Made in: U.S.A.
Value: $9.00 – 10.00
Description: Paper label on outside of plastic wrap reads "This limited edition collector's tin contains 8 oz. of Reese's peanut butter cups." The one on the bottom reads: "Classic Reese® Lunchbox."

Lunch Box (Rocky & Bullwinkle)

Category: Nonplastic
Contents: Candy, 3.8 oz.
Size: 4¹³⁄₁₆"h, 5⅝"w, 2⅜"d
Made for: American Specialty Confections, Inc., Lancaster, PA 17603
Made in: China
Cost new: $8.95 \ **Value:** $9.00 – 12.00
Description: Printed on the bottom of the box: "#38™ © 1997." The label on the back reads "This limited edition collector's tin may contain one or more of the following nostalgic candies: Butterscotch Buttons, Dubble Bubble®, Jolly Rancher®, Lemonheads®, Mary Janes®, Smarties®, Starlight Mints, or Tootsie Roll®. Net Wt. 3.8 oz."

Lurch (Addams Family)

Category: Characters
Contents: Pressed candy in skull-and-bones shapes, 0.28 oz.
Size: 4⅜"h, 2½"w, 1⅝"d
Made for: Bee International, Chula Vista, CA 91912
Made in: China
Value: $6.00 – 7.00
Description: Featuring Lurch, hulking character from the Addams Family. Embossed on the back: "© 1993 HBPC."

M&M's (dispenser)

Category: Characters
Contents: M&M's
Size: 9¼"h, 8⅝"w, 4½"d
Made for: M&M Mars, Division of Mars, Inc., Hackettstown, NJ 07804-1503
Made in: China
Cost new: $15.00 \ **Value:** $15.00 – 20.00
Description: Remove cap to refill with candy. On the bottom is embossed "CE © MARS INC. MADE IN CHINA not suitable for children under 36 months." Also embossed on the bottom is a picture of two M&M's characters with the words "The milk chocolate melts in your mouth – not in your hands. Official M&M's brand collectible."

M&M's (hook & ladder engine)

Category: Nonplastic
Contents: Candy, 10 oz.
Size: 5⁷⁄₁₆"h, 5⁷⁄₁₆"w, 4¼"d
Made for: M&M Mars Division of Mars, Inc., Hackettstown, NJ 07804-1503
Cost new: $3.59 \ **Value:** $3.50 – 4.50
Description: Tin container covered with clear plastic wrap, printed with M&M's plain chocolate candies. Printed on the bottom: "M&M's Brand Christmas Village Series. M&M's Brand Fire House, Number 06, Limited Edition Canister 1997." This limited edition collectible is the sixth in a series of M&M's brand canisters featuring the unique M&M's brand Christmas Village. Here the M&M's characters are busy making sure all is in order at the fire house. Has a picture of two M&M's with: "The milk chocolate melts in your mouth not in your hands." Official M&M's Brand.

M&M's (La-z-boy)

Category: Characters
Contents: M & M's peanut
Size: 8³⁄₁₆"h, 7"w, 10"d
Made for: M & M Mars, Division of Mars, Inc., Hackettstown, NJ 07804-1503
Made in: China
Cost new: $14.00 \ **Value:** $15.00 – 20.00
Description: "1. Fill dispenser with M&M's® Chocolate candies through the opening in the chair back. 2. Pull LA-Z-BOY chair lever down. 3. Candies are dispensed into your hand or, on the carpet." On the bottom is embossed "CE © MARS INC. MADE IN CHINA 'M' and the 'M&M' Character are registered trademarks of Mars, Incorporated. WARNING: CHOKING HAZARD. Small parts not for children under 3 years."

M&M's (Secret Santa Snow Globe)

Category: Holiday
Contents: M&M's
Size: 4¾"h, 2¾"w, 3¼"d
Made for: Mars, Inc., Hackettstown, NJ 07840-1503
Made in: China
Value: $6.00 – 7.50
Description: Embossed on the bottom: "CE © MARS INC. MADE IN CHINA – NOT SUITABLE FOR CHILDREN UNDER 36 MONTHS." Lift the M&M Santa and turn him upside down and little M&M's float around.

M&M's (with ears)

Category: Characters
Contents: M&M's Minis
Size: 4⅛"h, 2½"w, 2⅜"d
Made for: M&M Mars, Division of Mars, Inc., Hackettstown, NJ 07804-1503
Made in: China
Cost new: $0.99 \ **Value:** $2.00 – 3.00
Description: Has a baseball cap on backwards. Comes in different colors. Embossed on the bottom: "Warning: CHOKING HAZARD – Small parts. Not suitable for children under 36 months. Made in China – C3."

M&M's Minis

Category: Miscellaneous
Contents: M&M's Minis, 1.24 oz.
Size: 3¹⁵⁄₁₆"h, 1⁵⁄₁₆"w, 1⅝"d
Made for: Mars Inc., Hackettstown, NJ 07804-1503
Value: $1.00 – 1.50
Description: Has flip-top closure.

M&M's Peanut

Category: Characters
Contents: M&M's peanut
Size: 3⁹⁄₁₆"h, 3⅛"w, 1¾"d
Made for: Mars Inc., Hackettstown, NJ 07840-1503
Made in: China
Value: $2.50 – 3.50
Description: Part of a series of M&M's containers. This one is peanut. Embossed on the back: "© MARS, INC. 1991."

M&M's Plain

Category: Characters
Contents: M&M's plain
Size: 3⁵⁄₁₆"h, 3⅛"w, 1⅜"d
Made for: Mars Inc., Hackettstown, NJ 07840-1503
Made in: China
Value: $2.50 – 3.50
Description: Part of a series of standing, affable M&M's characters. © 1991.

M&M's Toys (Blue)

Category: Characters
Contents: M&M's fun-size pack
Size: 3¼"h, 1¹⁵⁄₁₆"w, 2³⁄₁₆"d
Made for: Burger King Corporation
Made in: China
Cost new: free w/kid's meal \ **Value:** $1.50 – 2.00
Description: Five in this Burger King kid's meal series. This one is Blue. Load M&M's through door on the back. Tilt body forward to dispense. © 1997.

M&M's Toys (Green)

Category: Characters
Contents: Candy, fun size pack
Size: 2½"h, 2"w, 2½"d
Made for: Burger King Corporation
Made in: China
Cost new: free w/kid's meal \ **Value:** $1.50 – 2.00
Description: There are five in the series, which were given away with a kid's meal at Burger King. This one is Green. Load M&M's candies through door on the back. Roll along to dispense. © Mars © 1997 Burger King Corporation.

M&M's Toys (Orange)

Category: Characters
Contents: Candy, fun size pack
Size: 2¾"h, 1¹⁵⁄₁₆"w, 3"d
Made for: Burger King Corporation
Made in: China
Cost new: free w/kid's meal \ **Value:** $1.50 – 2.00
Description: There are five in the series, which were given away with a kid's meal at Burger King. This one is Orange. Lift lid to load M&M's candies. Tilt bin to dump.

M&M's Toys (Red)

Category: Characters
Contents: Candy, fun size pack
Size: 1⅞"h, 2⅞"w
Made for: Burger King Corporation
Made in: China
Cost new: free w/kid's meal \ **Value:** $1.50 – 2.00
Description: There are five in the series, which were given away with a kid's meal at Burger King. This one is Red. Load M&M's candies through door on the back, turn body to dispense from inner tube. © Mars © 1997 Burger King Corporation.

M&M's Toys (Yellow)

Category: Characters
Contents: Candy, fun size pack
Size: 2½"h, 3"w, 2¼"d
Made for: Burger King Corporation
Made in: China
Cost new: free w/kid's meal \ **Value:** $1.50 – 2.00
Description: There are five in the series, which were given away with a kid's meal at Burger King. This one is Yellow. Load M&M's candies through door on the back. Roll along to dispense. © Mars © 1997 Burger King Corporation.

Magic

Category: Miscellaneous
Contents: Milk chocolate ball, 1.02 oz.
Size: 2½"h, 2⁷⁄₁₆"w, 2⁷⁄₁₆"d
Made for: Nestle USA, INC. Confection Div., Glendale, CA 91203
Made in: China
Value: $7.00 – 9.00
Description: This is a paper box with a milk chocolate ball, over a plastic ball, with Disney character inside. There are 24 different characters. On the box it says "Safety tested for kids of all ages," but it was taken off the market because it was considered unsafe.

Magic Picture

Category: Miscellaneous
Contents: Colored candy balls
Size: 4¾"h, 3⅝"w, ¹³⁄₁₆"d
Made for: Bee International, Chula Vista, CA 91912
Made in: China
Value: $4.00 – 5.00
Description: It has a stand on the back so it will sit upright on a flat surface and two holes to hang on a nail. Embossed on the back is "MADE IN CHINA." Comes on a card that reads "Magic Picture Candy Machine." Refillable candy dispenser. Net Wt. 0.3 oz.

Mailbox

Category: Miscellaneous
Contents: Candy, 0.4 oz.
Size: $2\frac{13}{16}$"h, $1\frac{3}{8}$"w, $1\frac{5}{16}$"d
Made for: Fleer Corp., Philadelphia, PA 19141
Made in: U.S.A.
Cost new: $0.49 \ **Value:** $2.50 – 3.50
Description: Embossed on closure is "MAIL."
On paper label: "FLEER, Full of Hearts."

Mailbox (Hershey's)

Category: Miscellaneous
Contents: Exact type unknown
Size: $3\frac{15}{16}$"h, $3\frac{5}{16}$"w, $5\frac{3}{4}$"d
Made for: Hershey Foods Corp.
Value: $10.50 – 15.50
Description: Mailbox is filled with Hershey's candy. Embossed on the bottom: "HERSHEY'S is a trademark of Hershey Foods Corporation, True Precision Plastic, licensee. © HERSHEY FOODS CORPORATION."

Mailbox (See's)

Category: Nonplastic
Contents: Suckers and chocolates, 7 oz.
Size: $3\frac{7}{8}$"h, $5\frac{7}{8}$"w, $3\frac{1}{4}$"d
Made for: See's Candy Shop Inc., Los Angeles, CA
Made in: China
Cost new: $5.75 \ **Value:** $6.00 – 7.50
Description: Made of tin with a plastic flag. Covered with clear plastic wrap and tied with a white ribbon. The ribbon has "See's Candies" written on it.

Mario

Category: Characters
Contents: Bubble gum, 0.8 oz.
Size: $3\frac{1}{8}$"h, $2\frac{3}{16}$"w, $1\frac{1}{4}$"d
Made for: Topps Co., Duryea, PA 18642
Made in: Taiwan
Value: $3.50 – 6.50
Description: Featuring Mario of Nintendo fame. Came in many colors. Embossed on the bottom: "© 1989 NOA."

Martian (tin)

Category: Nonplastic
Contents: Caramel bar, ⅞ oz.
Size: 4¹⁄₁₆"h, 2¹³⁄₁₆"w, 1⅞"d
Made for: Russell Stover Candies Inc., Kansas City, MO 64106
Made in: China
Cost new: $1.99 \ **Value:** $2.00 – 3.00
Description: Tin box. Looks like a Band-Aid box. On front is written: "Surprise Tin, Looney Tunes." On the back: "Surprise Tin, Collect all 5 Surprise Toys." Series featured Wile E. Coyote, Taz, Daffy Duck, Road Runner, and Bugs Bunny.

Mask

Category: Gumball dispensers
Contents: Jaw breakers, 1.75 oz.
Size: 5¾"h, 2⅛"w, 2⅜"d
Made for: Imagining 3, Niles, IL 60714
Made in: China
Value: $8.50 – 9.50
Description: Packaging reads "Collectible Candy Machine – Jawbreakers!" From the movie "The Mask." Embossed on the bottom: "Patents Pending PATS 5,385,267 D359, 232 made in China."

Max Headroom

Category: Characters
Contents: Colored tablets, 0.4 oz.
Size: 2⅜"h, 1⅜"w, 1⅞"d
Made for: The Topps Co. Inc., Duryea, PA 18642
Made in: Hong Kong
Value: $15.00 – 18.00
Description: Screw closure on the bottom. Paper label reads "© 1987 Chrysalis Visual Programming Ltd. All rights reserved."

Maze Candy (X-Men)

Category: Games
Contents: Gum, 2 oz.
Size: 4"h, 3⅜"w, 1¼"d
Made for: Classic Heroes Inc., Stuart, FL 34995
Made in: China
Cost new: $1.59 \ **Value:** $3.00 – 4.00
Description: Based on the X-Men comic. Item No. 57000. © 1995.

McNugget Buddy (McDonald's)

Category: Characters
Contents: Nerds
Size: 2⅝"h, 2⅛"w, 1⅞"d
Made for: McDonald's Corp., Oak Brook, IL 60521
Made in: China
Cost new: free w/Happy Meal \ **Value:** $1.00 – 2.00
Description: Marketed as McDonald's Happy Meal toy. One of a series of six. This one is #4. Plastic wrap has messages in English, French, and Spanish. It comes with a separate bag of Wonka Spooky Nerds candy. You can lift the mask on the container to see the character and put the candy in. The mask is the closure. Also there is a spring loaded door on the bottom. Embossed on the back of the container is "© 1998 McDonald's Corp. China/Chine TW 13."

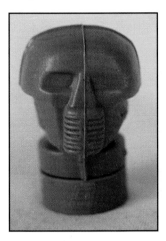

Medical Droid 2-1B (Empire Strikes Back)

Category: Characters
Contents: Colored pellets, 0.5 oz.
Size: 2⁷⁄₁₆"h, 1⅝"w, 1⅝"d
Made for: Topps Co., Duryea, PA
Made in: Hong Kong
Value: $4.00 – 6.00
Description: Embossed on the closure: "Star Wars: The Empire Strikes Back." © 1980. To get the candy out, turn closure to hole in container.

Meg (Hercules)

Category: Gumball dispensers
Contents: Gumballs, 0.8 oz.
Size: 6¼"h, 1⅝"w, 1½"d
Made for: Imagining 3, Niles, IL 60714
Made in: China
Cost new: $1.57 \ **Value:** $3.50 – 4.50
Description: From the Disney movie "Hercules." Label reads "Flix, Disney's Hercules, Candy Machine. For ages 3 and up."

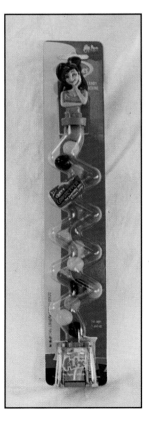

Meg (candy machine)

Category: Gumball dispensers
Contents: Gobstoppers, 2.48 oz.
Size: 12½"h, 2"w, 1⅜"d
Made for: Imagining 3, Niles, IL 60714
Made in: China
Value: $3.50 – 4.50
Description: Candy machine from Disney's "Hercules." Pat. 5,385,267 – D359, 232. Label reads "Flix, Disney's Hercules, Candy Machine. For ages 3 and up."

Michael Jordan (Space Jam)

Category: Characters
Contents: Gumballs
Size: 5⅛"h, 2⁹/₁₆"w, 2⅜"d
Made for: Warner Brothers
Made in: Mexico
Cost new: $2.59 \ **Value:** $4.00 – 6.00
Description: Bust of Michael Jordan with "Space Jam" written on front. Inside were Trophy Treats, basketball-shaped gumballs. © 1996.

Michael's Secret Stuff

Category: Bottles and jars
Contents: Blue powder candy
Size: 5½"h, 1¾"w
Made for: Creative Confection Concepts, Milwaukee, WI 53209
Made in: Mexico
Value: $2.00 – 3.00
Description: From the "Space Jam" movie. Closure is screw-on with pull top. Embossed on the bottom: "™ © 1996 WARNER BROS. made in Mexico."

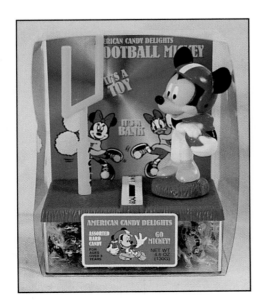

Mickey Football

Category: Characters
Contents: Fruit flavored candy, 4.6 oz.
Size: 6½"h, 5"w, 3"d
Made for: American Candy Co. Inc., Selma, AL 36701
Made in: China
Cost new: $3.00 \ **Value:** $5.00 – 6.00
Description: Moveable three-piece action figure and goal post. It has a coin slot to be used as a bank. Mickey is made of soft plastic and is in three pieces so you can move it in different positions.

Mickey Mouse (Mickey's stuff)

Category: Characters
Contents: Gumballs, 0.45 oz.
Size: 3¾"h, 2¾"w, 1⅝"d
Made for: Leaf Inc., Lake Forest, IL 60045
Made in: China
Cost new: $2.29 \ **Value:** $3.00 – 4.50
Description: ASI#4941625-A. Comes on a card with a hole in it to operate. Mickey is dressed as a pirate, standing next to a treasure chest. Colored gumballs have Mickey's outline printed on them. Comes in a series of four: Mickey Mouse, Minnie Mouse, Goofy, and Donald Duck. © Disney.

Milk Can

Category: Nonplastic
Contents: Butter toffee, 8 oz.
Size: 6⁷⁄₁₆"h, 3¹¹⁄₁₆"w
Made for: Smith Enterprises, Inc., Rock Hill, SC 29731
Cost new: $2.97 \ **Value:** $3.00 – 4.00
Description: Made out of tin. Has a paper tag attached with an elastic cord. Front of the tag reads "Dairy Delites. Butter Toffee Candy. Net. Wt. 8 oz. (226 g)." It also has a picture of a barnyard with cows, chickens, barn, and silo. Candy made in Argentina. The container is sealed with clear plastic wrap.

Minnie Mouse (Mickey's stuff)

Category: Characters
Contents: Gumballs, 0.45 oz.
Size: 3⅜"h, 2⅞"w, 1¼"d
Made for: Leaf Inc., Lake Forest, IL 60045
Made in: China
Cost new: $2.29 \ **Value:** $3.00 – 4.00
Description: ASI#4941626-A. Comes on a card with a hole in it to operate. Minnie is leaning on a juke box with a record in her hand. Colored gumballs have Mickey's outline printed on them. Comes in a series of four: Mickey Mouse, Minnie Mouse, Goofy, and Donald Duck. © Disney.

Monster (head)

Category: Characters
Contents: Small colored balls
Size: 2⁵⁄₁₆"h, 2⅜"w, 1⅞"d
Made in: China
Value: $4.00 – 5.50
Description: Has a ring on top with string. Inside was small package of candy and paper stickers. Embossed on closure: "Made in China."

Monster Mouth (Dracula)

Category: Characters
Contents: Candy tongue, 0.67 oz.
Size: 2"h, 1¹⁵⁄₁₆"w, 7"d
Made for: Cap Toys Inc., Bedford Heights, OH 44146
Made in: China
Cost new: $1.99 \ **Value:** $2.50 – 3.50
Description: Has blood on teeth, pointed ears and fangs. Patent No. 5,531,318. If you pull back, mouth opens and candy tongue comes out. Part of series.

Monster Mouth (Frankenstein)

Category: Characters
Contents: Candy tongue, 0.67 oz.
Size: 2"h, 1⁵⁄₁₆"w, 7"d
Made for: Cap Toys Inc., Bedford Heights, OH 44146
Made in: China
Cost new: $1.99 \ **Value:** $2.50 – 3.50
Description: Has monster head on end. Pull back and mouth opens and tongue comes out. Patent No. 5,531,318.

Monster Mouth (Godzilla)

Category: Animals
Contents: Candy tongue, 0.67 oz.
Size: 1½"h, 1¹³⁄₁₆"w, 8⅛"l
Made for: Oddzon Inc., Bedford Hts., OH 44146
Made in: China
Cost new: $1.99 \ **Value:** $2.50 – 3.50
Description: Has monster head on end. Pull back and mouth opens and tongue comes out. Patent No. 5,531,318. Godzilla and Godzilla character design are trademarks of Toho Co., Ltd. © 1998 Toho Co., All rights reserved.

Monster Mouth (Mummy)

Category: Characters
Contents: Candy tongue, 0.67 oz.
Size: 2"h, 1¹³⁄₁₆"w, 6⅝"d
Made for: Cap Toys Inc., Bedford Heights, OH 44146
Made in: China
Cost New: $1.99 \ **Value:** $2.50 – 3.50
Description: Tongue pops out when head is pulled back. Part of a series. Patent No. 5,531,318.

Motorcycle (See's)

Category: Nonplastic
Contents: Assorted See's candies
Size: 3⅞"h, 4½"w, 6⅜"d
Made for: See's Candy, Los Angeles, CA
Made in: China
Cost new: $10.00 \ **Value:** $10.00 – 14.00
Description: Made of tin and pot metal, driver is plastic.
Front compartment and back doors open.

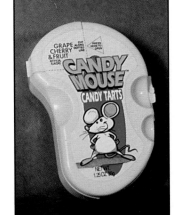

Mouse (computer)

Category: Miscellaneous
Contents: Candy tarts, 1.25 oz.
Size: 1⅛"h, 2⅜"w, 3¾"d (without tail), tail is 3¾"
Made for: Amurol Confection Co., Yorkville, IL 60560
Made in: Canada
Cost new: $0.97 \ **Value:** $1.50 – 2.00
Description: Front label has picture of a mouse standing with
hands on hips. Has rubber tail coming out of the bottom.

Mouse (Jerry)

Category: Characters
Contents: Pill-shaped candy
Size: 3⅝"h, 2⅓"w, 1⅝"d
Made for: Bee International, Chula Vista, CA 91912
Made in: China
Value: $7.00 – 8.00
Description: This is Jerry from the characters Tom & Jerry. The label on the container
reads "© 1993 T.E.C. & Telefilm-Essen Gmbh. All Rights Reserved." Tom & Jerry The
Movie ™ are trademarks of Turner Entertainment Co. The candy has the name Tom on
some and Jerry on others. Embossed on the back of the head is "© 1993 T.E.C."

Mowgli (Jungle Book)

Category: Characters
Contents: Nerds
Size: 3"h, 2¹¹⁄₁₆"w, 2"d
Made for: McDonald's Corp., Oak Brook, IL 60521
Made in: China
Cost new: free w/Happy Meal \ **Value:** $2.00 – 3.00
Description: Part of Jungle Book series of toys that came in
Happy Meals. Embossed on the back: "MFG. FOR McD CORP.
© DISNEY CHINA CB CHINE."

Mr. Freeze

Category: Characters
Contents: White pressed candy, 3.5 oz.
Size: 4"h, 4"w, 2¼"d
Made for: Creative Confection Concepts, Milwaukee, WI 53209
Made in: China
Cost new: $2.29 \ **Value:** $5.00 – 6.50
Description: Label tied around the neck that reads "Mr. Freeze, candy." Inside label: "We aim to freeze! with a really COOL TASTE!" Embossed on the back: "made in Mexico ™& © 1997 DC COMICS."

Mr. & Mrs. Potato Head (Toy Story 2)

Category: Characters
Contents: Tart 'n Tinys
Size: 4⅝"h, 3¾"w, 3¼"d
Made for: McDonald's Corp., Oak Brook, IL 60521
Made in: China
Cost new: $2.50 \ **Value:** $3.00 – 5.00
Description: Embossed on his back is "Mfg. for McD Corp. China/Chine GG 01 © 1999 Hasbro, Inc." This is also a wind-up toy. It has an extra face. Net Wt. 1.5 oz. Chewy Tart 'n Tinys. One in a series of six.

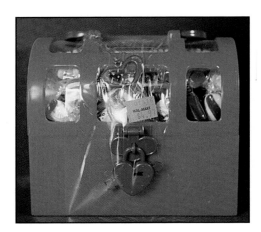

My Box

Category: Miscellaneous
Contents: Assorted
Size: 5¼"h, 6"w, 4"d
Made for: The Jelly Bean Factory, Fairfax, OH 45227
Made in: China
Cost new: $4.97 \ **Value:** $5.00 – 6.50
Description: Looks like a lunch box or treasure chest with padlock on front. Embossed with "My Box" and two hearts. Padlock has arrow through it. Key hangs from a gold string tied to the handle. Can be used as a bank.

Ninja Head (Donatello sewer)

Category: Characters
Contents: Colored pellets
Size: 1¹³⁄₁₆"h, 1¹¹⁄₁₆"w, 1¹¹⁄₁₆"d
Made for: The Topps Co. Inc., Duryea, PA 18642
Made in: China
Value: $4.00 – 6.00
Description: Donatello coming out of a manhole. Embossed on the manhole ring is "CITY SEWER Donatello." Embossed on the closure: "© 1991 Mirage Studios Inc."

Ninja Head (Michaelangelo sewer)

Category: Characters
Contents: Colored pellets
Size: 1¹³⁄₁₆"h, 1¹¹⁄₁₆"w, 1¹¹⁄₁₆"d
Made for: The Topps Co. Inc., Duryea, PA 18642
Made in: China
Value: $4.00 – 6.00
Description: Michaelangelo coming out of a manhole. Embossed on manhole ring is "CITY SEWER Michaelangelo." Embossed on the closure: "© 1991 Mirage Studios Inc."

Ninja Head (Raphael sewer)

Category: Characters
Contents: Colored pellets
Size: 1¹³⁄₁₆"h, 1¹¹⁄₁₆"w, 1¹¹⁄₁₆"d
Made for: The Topps Co., Duryea, PA 18642
Made in: China
Value: $4.00 – 6.00
Description: Raphael coming out of a manhole. Embossed on manhole ring is "CITY SEWER RAPHAEL." © 1991. Mirage Studios Inc.

Ninja Turtle (Donatello)

Category: Characters
Contents: Gum, 0.3 oz.
Size: 2¹³⁄₁₆"h, 1⅝"w, 1⅜"d
Made for: The Topps Co. Inc., Duryea, PA 18642
Made in: Taiwan
Value: $3.00 – 4.00
Description: Part of a Ninja Turtle container series. Embossed on the closure: "Donatello. Made in Taiwan © 1990 MIRAGE STUDIOS, USA."

Ninja Turtle (Leonardo)

Category: Characters
Contents: Gum, 0.3 oz.
Size: 2⅞"h, 1¾"w, 1"d
Made for: Mirage Studios, U.S.A
Made in: Taiwan
Value: $3.00 – 4.00
Description: Part of a Ninja Turtle container series. Embossed on the closure: "LEONARDO. Made in Taiwan © 1990 MIRAGE STUDIOS, USA."

Ninja Turtle (Michaelangelo)

Category: Characters
Contents: Gum, 0.3 oz.
Size: 2¹³⁄₁₆"h, 1¾"w, 1½"d
Made for: Topps Co., Duryea, PA 19642
Made in: Taiwan
Value: $3.00 – 4.00
Description: Part of the Ninja Turtle series. Embossed on the bottom: "Michaelangelo Made in Taiwan © 1990 Mirage Studios, USA."

Ninja Turtle (Raphael)

Category: Characters
Contents: Gum, 0.3 oz.
Size: 2¾"h, 1¹³⁄₁₆"w, 1¹⁄₁₆"d
Made for: Topps Co., Duryea, PA 19642
Made in: Taiwan
Value: $3.00 – 4.00
Description: Part of the Ninja Turtle series. Embossed on the bottom: "Raphael Made in Taiwan © 1990 Mirage Studios, USA."

Orange

Category: Food items
Contents: Powder, ⅝ oz.
Size: 2⅝"h, 1⅝"w
Made for: Ce De Candy Inc., Union, NJ 07083
Made in: U.S.A.
Cost new: $0.40 \ **Value:** $1.00 – 2.00
Description: Came with a paper label under the screw cap. Cap has ring for a string.

Pacifier (Bib Baby Shakes)

Category: Miscellaneous
Contents: Gum, 1.5 oz.
Size: 3¾"h (handle extended), 2¹¹⁄₁₆"w, 2¼"d
Made for: Albert & Son, Inc., Greenwich, CT 06830
Made in: China
Cost new: $1.19 \ **Value:** $2.00 – 3.00
Description: Rubber nipple on top. Picture of a kid with a cap labeled "CANDY." The nipple is located where the nose would be. Has a plastic lanyard. To be worn around the neck.

Pacifier (big ring)

Category: Miscellaneous
Contents: Gum
Size: 3¾"h, 2¹⁄₁₆"w
Cost new: $0.95 \ **Value:** $2.50 – 3.50
Description: Came with a blue plastic cord to be worn around the neck. Purchased in Yuma, Arizona, in 1996. No label or markings.

Pacifier (large closure)

Category: Miscellaneous
Contents: Small colored beads
Size: 3⁵⁄₁₆"h, 1⁹⁄₁₆"w
Cost new: $0.65 \ **Value:** $2.50 – 3.50
Description: No label and no markings. Opening in large top pacifier is smaller than opening in small top pacifier. Came with a yellow cord and in other colors.

Pacifier (small closure)

Category: Miscellaneous
Contents: Colored beads, 0.30 oz.
Size: 2¾"h, 1¼"w
Made for: Novelty Specialties Inc., Campbell, CA
Made in: Taiwan
Cost new: $0.65 \ **Value:** $2.50 – 3.50
Description: Came with a pink cord to be worn around the neck. Screw-top closure. Assorted colors.

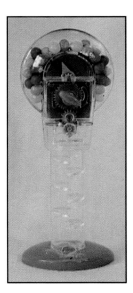

Parking Meter

Category: Miscellaneous
Contents: Colored candy balls
Size: 5½"h, 2⅛"w, 1¾"d
Made for: Bee International, Chula Vista, CA 91912
Made in: China
Cost new: $1.99 \ **Value:** $4.00 – 5.00
Description: Embossed on the front of the meter is "SHAKE BEFORE USE." On the bottom is © 1998 Sunco – Patent Pending – Made in China." It comes on a card that reads "REFILLABLE – CRAZY CANDY PARKING METER WITH SPIRAL DISPENSING ACTION." Net Wt. 0.5 oz. Filled with Concord Mini Micro Bytes. It has a door on the back for refilling.

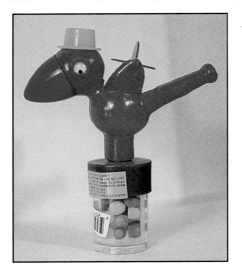

Parrot Whistle

Category: Animals
Contents: Colored candy beads
Size: 4⅝"h, 1⁵⁄₁₆"w, 3⅞"d
Made for: Allen Mitchell Products, Oxnard, CA 93030
Made in: Hong Kong
Cost new: $0.59 \ **Value:** $5.00 – 7.00
Description: Eyes move when shaken and wheel spins when whistle blown. Clear bottom sides are prism-like. Hat has hole in its top.

Pelon Pelo Rico

Category: Miscellaneous
Contents: Tamarind, 1 oz.
Size: 4"h, 2¹⁄₁₆"w, 1½"d
Made for: Lorena Mexican Products Inc., Otay Mesa, CA 92173
Made in: Mexico
Cost new: $0.50 \ **Value:** $2.00 – 3.00
Description: Syringe-style container. Label features a clown with big bow tie. Purchased in Yuma, Arizona, in 1996.

Pen (Candy Writer Necklace)

Category: Crayons, pencils, and pens
Contents: Colored candy beads, 0.63 oz.
Size: 6⅛"h, ¹⁵⁄₁₆"w
Made for: Goodlite Products Inc., Bedford, TX 76021
Made in: China
Cost new: $0.79 \ **Value:** $3.50 – 5.00
Description: Label calls this a Candy Writer Necklace. Item No. FT20250. Came with an orange cord. Pen really works.

Pen (PowerPenz)

Category: Crayons, pencils, and pens
Contents: Gobstoppers, 0.9 oz.
Size: 5¾"h, 1½"w, 1¼"d
Made for: Yes! Entertainment Corp., Pleasanton, CA 94588
Made in: China
Value: $3.00 – 4.00
Description: Writes in black ink. Cleaning and operating instructions on the back. © 1997. Label reads "Yes! is a registered trademark and HANDY CANDY, POWERPENZ and YES! GEAR are trademarks of YES! Entertainment Corp." SKU #940058.

Pen (PowerPenz 2)

Category: Crayons, pencils, and pens
Contents: Sweet Tarts, 0.72 oz.
Size: 5½"h, 1⅜"w, 1¼"d
Made for: Yes! Entertainment Corp., Pleasanton, CA 94588
Made in: China
Value: $3.00 – 4.00
Description: Embossed on center of the container: "PowerPenz Handy Candy." Made in 1997. SKU #940072.

Pencil Holder

Category: Crayons, pencils, and pens
Contents: Super bubble gum, 1.5 oz.
Size: 9⅛"h, 1³⁄₁₆"w, 1⅜"d
Made for: Leaf Inc., Lake Forest, IL 60045
Made in: Taiwan

Cost new: $2.49 \ **Value:** $3.00 – 4.00
Description: Embossed on the top: "Made in Taiwan." It is made to be used as a pen or pencil holder. It has a pencil sharpener on the end. Came with three sticks of bubble gum.

Pencil Sharpener

Category: Nonplastic
Contents: Jelly Belly, 3 oz.
Size: 5"h, 2¼"w
Made for: Herman Goelitz Candy Co. Inc., Fairfield, CA 94533
Made in: China
Cost new: $2.97 \ **Value:** $3.00 – 4.00
Description: Made of tin. Has a pencil sharpener on the top of the container. Is filled with five twist wrapped flavors. Jelly Belly jelly beans Sours.

Pickle (Piccolo)

Category: Food items
Contents: Gum, 0.5 oz.
Size: 3¼"h, 1⅛"w, 1¹⁄₁₆"d
Made for: Creative Confection Concepts, Milwaukee, WI 53209
Made in: Mexico
Cost new: $0.69 \ **Value:** $4.00 – 6.00
Description: Whistle, toy, and bubblegum container in one. Has a plastic cord.

Pickle Puss

Category: Food items
Contents: Bubble gum, 1.7 oz.
Size: 5½"h, 1⅜"w
Made for: Creative Confection Concepts, Milwaukee, WI 53209
Made in: Mexico
Cost new: $0.69 \ **Value:** $4.00 – 6.00
Description: Filled with pickle-flavored gum. Closure is screw-cap. Came with plastic lace for carrying.

Pick'n Chews (nose)

Category: Miscellaneous
Contents: Bubble gum, 0.3 oz.
Size: 2⅛"h, 1⅜"w, 1¼"d
Made for: The Topps Co. Inc., Duryea, PA 18642
Made in: China
Value: $7.00 – 8.50
Description: It has a ring on the back to put your finger in. With your other finger you tilt the nose back and the candy comes out of the nostrils. Comes on a card labeled "Pick'n Chew." Also comes on cards with different faces. Directions are on the back. #536 Candies made in Hong Kong. © 1989

Pig (Candy Pet)

Category: Animals
Contents: Colored candy beads
Size: 2⅞"h, 1¹³⁄₁₆"w, 1½"d
Made for: Wizard Toys Inc., Bell, CA 90201
Made in: China
Value: $3.00 – 4.00
Description: There are six different Wizard Candy Pets: Bear, Cat, Chick, Dog, Duck, and Pig. They are sold on a card. Net Wt. 1 oz. The hat is the closure. Candy made in Canada. Item 7100.

Pig (Hamilton)

Category: Animals
Contents: Sugarless candy, 0.2 oz.
Size: 2⅝"h, 2"w, 1⁷⁄₁₆"d
Made for: Topps Co., Duryea, PA 18642
Made in: China
Cost new: $0.99 \ **Value:** $4.00 – 6.00
Description: Hamilton the Pig, from Tiny Toon Adventures. Made in 1991.

Pig (Hamm, Toy Story 2)

Category: Characters
Contents: Candy on paper
Size: 3"h, 2⅝"w, 5"d
Made for: McDonald's Corp., Oak Brook, IL 60521
Made in: China
Cost new: $2.50 \ **Value:** $3.00 – 5.00
Description: Embossed inside the pig is "Mfg. for McD Corp. China/Chine WH 02 © 1999 McDonald's Corp. © Disney." One in a series of six. Twist the tail and the ears move.

Pig (piggy bank)

Category: Animals
Contents: Heart Breakers, 6 oz.
Size: 2⅞"h, 2⅝"w, 3¹¹⁄₁₆"d
Made for: The Jelly Bean Factory, Fairfax, OH 45227
Made in: China
Cost new: $1.97 \ **Value:** $2.50 – 3.00
Description: Bank is filled with heart-shaped candy.

Pig (sitting)

Category: Animals
Contents: Colored candy beads, ⅜ oz.
Size: 3⅛"h, 1⅞"w, 1¾"d
Made for: E. Rosen Company, Pawtucket, RI
Made in: U.S.A.
Value: $7.00 – 8.50
Description: The only closure is the Scotch tape over the opening. A #5 is located on back of the head and a curly tail at the rear end. The label on the back has no zip code.

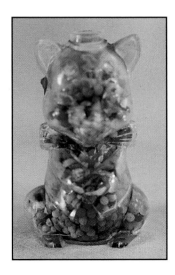

Pineapple

Category: Food items
Contents: Powdered candy, ⅝ oz.
Size: 2¹³⁄₁₆"h, 1¾"w
Made for: Ce De Candy Inc., Union, NJ 07083
Made in: U.S.A.
Cost new: $0.40 \ **Value:** $1.00 – 1.50
Description: Cap has ring for a string. Paper label under the screw cap.

Pluggo

Category: Characters
Contents: Colored candy pills
Size: 2⅛"h, 1⅝"w, 1¹¹⁄₁₆"d
Made for: The Topps Co., Duryea, PA 18642
Made in: China
Value: $5.00 – 7.00
Description: These come in different colors and different hairdos. The plug in the belly is the closure. Pull the plug to get the candy. Embossed on the back is "© 1986 TOPPS CHEWING GUM INC."

Pocket Pal (alligator)

Category: Animals
Contents: Bubble gumballs, 0.5 oz.
Size: 6¾"h, 1"w, 1⅛"d
Made for: Hilco Corporation, Norristown, PA 19401
Made in: China
Cost new: $0.97 \ **Value:** $2.00 – 3.00
Description: This container is made to put in your pocket like a pen. Has a clip to hold it. Comes in different animals. Open the mouth to dispense gumballs. Embossed under the head: "Hilco Corporation © 1997 Made in China."

Pocket Pal (beaked animal)

Category: Animals
Contents: Bubble gumballs, 0.5 oz.
Size: 6⅝"h, 1¹⁄₁₆"w, 1¼"d
Made for: Hilco Corporation, Norristown, PA 19401
Made in: China
Cost new: $0.97 \ **Value:** $2.00 – 3.00

Description: This container is made to put in your pocket like a pen. Has a clip to hold it. Comes in different animals. Open the mouth to dispense gumballs. Embossed under the head: "Hilco Corporation © 1997 Made in China."

Pocket Pal (elephant)

Category: Animals
Contents: Bubble gumballs, 0.5 oz.
Size: 6¾"h, 1⅛"w, 1¼"d
Made for: Hilco Corporation, Norristown, PA 19401
Made in: China
Cost new: $0.97 \ **Value:** $2.00 – 3.00
Description: This container is made to put in your pocket like a pen. Has a clip to hold it. Comes in different animals. Open the mouth to dispense gumballs. Embossed under the head: "Hilco Corporation © 1997 Made in China."

Pocket Pal (hippo)

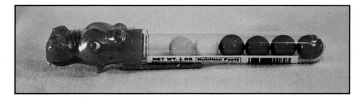

Category: Animals
Contents: Bubble gumballs, 0.5 oz.
Size: 6⅝"h, 1¼"w, 1¼"d
Made for: Hilco Corporation, Norristown, PA 19401
Made in: China
Cost new: $0.97 \ **Value:** $2.00 – 3.00

Description: This container is made to put in your pocket like a pen. Has a clip to hold it. Comes in different animals. Open the mouth to dispense gumballs. Embossed under the head: "Hilco Corporation © 1997 Made in China."

Pocket Pumper 49ers

Category: Miscellaneous
Contents: Candy tart
Size: 4¾"h, 1¹¹⁄₁₆"w, 2⅛"d
Made for: Illinoy Toy Co., Glenview, IL 60025
Made in: Canada
Value: $3.00 – 4.00
Description: Officially licensed NFL product. Comes in all the teams. To use, push down on the helmet and candy drops out. It is package on a card.

Poison Ivy

Category: Characters
Contents: Powdered candy, 1.3 oz.
Size: 3⅝"h, 3⁹⁄₁₆"w, ¹⁵⁄₁₆"d
Made for: Creative Confection Concepts, Milwaukee, WI 53209
Made in: Mexico
Cost new: $1.19 \ **Value:** $4.50 – 6.00
Description: Leaf-shaped container featuring Poison Ivy from the movie "Batman & Robin." Came with a plastic cord. Embossed on the top: "Made in Mexico™ & © 1997 DC COMICS."

Pokémon (Pikachu)

Category: Characters
Contents: Gum
Size: 3¾"h, 2⁷⁄₁₆"w, 1¹³⁄₁₆"d
Cost new: $1.00 \ **Value:** $3.00 – 4.00
Description: The only markings on the container are "#14" embossed backwards on the closure and a "V" indented under the left foot. I purchased this container new at a flea market in Yuma, Arizona, without any label or marking. I believe it was made in Mexico.

Pop Shots

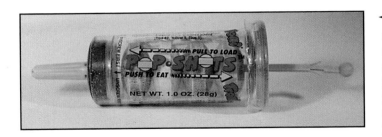

Category: Miscellaneous
Contents: Pressed candy, 1oz.
Size: 6"h, 1¾"w
Made for: Trolli Inc., Plantation, FL 33324
Made in: China
Cost new: $1.99 \ **Value:** $3.50 – 4.50
Description: Container looks like a hypodermic needle. Patent No. 5,222,627.

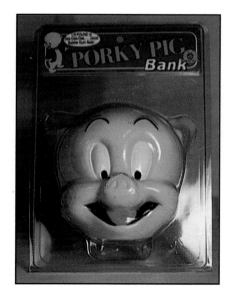

Porky Pig (bank)

Category: Characters
Contents: Gum, 5.3 oz.
Size: 4½"h, 4½"w, 4⅞"d
Made for: Creative Confection Concepts, Milwaukee, WI 53209
Made in: China
Cost new: $4.99 \ **Value:** $8.00 – 12.00
Description: Doubles as a bank. Push-in closure on bottom. Embossed around the closure: "™ & © 1997 WARNER BROS. made in China Creative Confection Concepts."

Potato Head

Category: Characters
Contents: Candy, 1 oz.
Size: 3¼"h, 2⅛"w, 2"d
Made for: Hasbro, Inc., Pawtucket, RI 02862
Made in: China
Cost new: $1.25 \ **Value:** $2.00 – 3.00
Description: His arms are painted white on the front, but not on the back. Comes covered with clear plastic wrap. Embossed on the back: "1996 Hasbro, Pawtucket, RI 02862. All rights reserved. Made in China."

Power Candy (M&M's)

Category: Battery operated
Contents: Plain M&M's, 1.47 oz.
Size: 4"w, 2"d
Made for: Cap Toys Inc., Bedford Heights, OH 44146
Made in: China
Value: $5.00 – 6.00
Description: Container looks like a flying saucer. Put candies in, press button on back, and inside of the container goes around and out pops candy. Uses one AAA battery. Has blue belt loops, yellow back, white middle, and red front with big white M on it.

Power Hose

Category: Nonplastic
Contents: Cherry liquid, 5 oz.
Size: 7⅛"h, 1¾"w
Made for: Amurol Confections Co., Yorkville, IL 60560
Made in: U.S.A.
Value: $2.00 – 3.00
Description: Aerosol can filled with liquid candy. © 1994.

Power Prism

Category: Miscellaneous
Contents: Colored candy balls, 0.7 oz.
Size: 3"h, 1¹⁵⁄₁₆"w
Made for: Creative Confection Concepts, Milwaukee, WI 53209
Value: $5.50 – 7.00
Description: Container becomes prism toy once candy is gone. Came with red plastic lace cord for carrying.

Power Ranger (bust, Billy)

Category: Characters
Contents: Jelly beans
Size: 3⅞"h, 3⅛"w, 1¹⁵⁄₁₆"d
Made for: Topps Co., Duryea, PA 18642
Made in: China
Cost new: $0.97 \ **Value:** $5.00 – 7.00
Description: Part of the Power Rangers series. Billy's helmet has horns pointing forward and two gold marks like eyes above the eye shield. His insignia is a triceratops. Embossed on the back: "™ and © 1993 SABAN" and "Made in China."

Power Ranger (bust, Jason)

Category: Characters
Contents: Jelly beans
Size: 3⅞"h, 3⅛"w, 1¹⁵⁄₁₆"d
Made for: Topps Co., Duryea, PA 18642
Made in: China
Cost new: $0.97 \ **Value:** $5.00 – 7.00
Description: Part of a Power Rangers series. Jason's helmet is red with teeth on sides of the eye shield. Has two black marks like eyes above teeth. Insignia is a T-Rex. Embossed on the back: "™© 1993 SABAN" and "Made in China."

Power Ranger (bust, Kimberly)

Category: Characters
Contents: Jelly beans
Size: 3¾"h, 3⅛"w, 1¹⁵⁄₁₆"d
Made for: Topps Co., Duryea, PA 18642
Made in: China
Cost new: $0.97 \ **Value:** $5.00 – 7.00
Description: Part of Power Rangers series. Kimberly's helmet has wedge in the middle of the eye lens. Has two small green dots resembling bird's nose. Insignia is a pterodactyl. Embossed on the back: "™© 1993 SABAN" and "Made in China."

Power Ranger (bust, Trini)

Category: Characters
Contents: Jelly beans
Size: 3⅞"h, 3⅛"w, 1¹⁵⁄₁₆"d
Made for: Topps Co., Duryea, PA 18642
Made in: China
Cost new: $0.97 \ **Value:** $5.00 – 7.00
Description: Part of Power Rangers series. Trini's helmet has a big tooth coming down over the eye lens on each side. Two black spots above each tooth resemble eyes. Insignia is a saber-tooth tiger. Embossed on the back: "™© 1993 SABAN" and "Made in China."

Power Ranger (bust, Zack)

Category: Characters
Contents: Jelly beans
Size: 3⅞"h, 3⅛"w, 1¹⁵⁄₁₆"d
Made for: Topps Co., Duryea, PA 18642
Made in: China
Cost new: $0.97 \ **Value:** $5.00 – 7.00
Description: Part of Power Rangers series. Zack's helmet is black with horns coming down and two gold spots like eyes on top. Insignia on the chest is a mammoth. Embossed on the back: "™© 1993 SABAN" and "Made in China."

Power Ranger (Flix, Billy)

Category: Gumball dispensers
Contents: Gumballs, 0.8 oz.
Size: 5"h, 1½"w, 1⅝"d
Made for: Imagining 3, Niles, IL 60714
Made in: China
Value: $8.50 – 10.00
Description: Embossed on the bottom: "Made in China Patents Pending." Front of the package reads "Pocket Candy Machine – Diamond – Collectible – Flix Mighty Morphin Power Rangers™." Embossed on lower front: "Flix." This is the first series. Comes on a blue card.

Power Ranger (Flix, Jason)

Category: Gumball dispensers
Contents: Gumballs, 0.8 oz.
Size: 5"h, 1½"w, 1⅝"d
Made for: Imagining 3, Niles, IL 60714
Made in: China
Value: $8.50 – 10.00
Description: Front label reads "Pocket Candy Machine – Collectible – Diamond – Flix Mighty Morphin Power Rangers." This is the first series. Comes on a blue card.

Power Ranger (Flix, Kim)

Category: Gumball dispensers
Contents: Gumballs, 0.8 oz.
Size: 5"h, 1½"w, 1⅝"d
Made for: Imagining 3, Niles, IL 60714
Made in: China
Value: $8.50 – 10.00
Description: Embossed on the bottom: "Made In China Patents Pending." Front of package reads "Pocket Candy Machine – Diamond – Collectible – Flix Mighty Morphin Power Rangers™." Embossed on lower front: "Flix." This is the first series. Comes on a blue card.

Power Ranger (Flix, Trini)

Category: Gumball dispensers
Contents: Gumballs, 0.8 oz.
Size: 5"h, 1½"w, 1⅝"d
Made for: Imagining 3, Niles, IL 60714
Made in: China
Value: $8.50 – 10.00
Description: Part of a series. Front label: "Pocket Candy Machine – Collectible – Diamond – Flix Mighty Morphin Power Rangers." Embossed on the bottom: "Made in China Patents Pending." This is the first series. Comes on a blue card.

Power Ranger (Flix, Zack)

Category: Gumball dispensers
Contents: Gumballs, 0.8 oz.
Size: 5⅛"h, 1½"w, 1⅝"d
Made for: Imagining 3, Niles, IL 60714
Made in: China
Value: $15.50 – 18.50
Description: Part of a series of Power Ranger pocket candy machines. Embossed on the bottom: "Made in China Patents Pending." This is the first series. Comes on a blue card.

Power Ranger (head, Billy)

Category: Characters
Contents: Candy, 0.4 oz.
Size: 2¼"h, 1¹⁵⁄₁₆"w, 2³⁄₁₆"d
Made for: Topps Co., Duryea, PA 18642
Made in: China
Cost new: $1.09 \ **Value:** $4.00 – 5.00
Description: Whole container is a helmet. Only the mouth shows. Embossed on the back: "™© 1995 Saban." Came with clear plastic wrap with ingredients written on it.

Power Ranger (head, Jason)

Category: Characters
Contents: Candy, 0.4 oz.
Size: 2¼"h, 1¹⁵⁄₁₆"w, 2³⁄₁₆"d
Made for: Topps Co., Duryea, PA 18642
Made in: China
Cost new: $1.09 \ **Value:** $4.00 – 5.00
Description: Whole container is a helmet. Only the mouth shows. Embossed on the back: "™© 1995 Saban." Came with clear plastic wrap with ingredients written on it.

Power Ranger (head, Kimberly)

Category: Characters
Contents: Candy, 0.4 oz.
Size: 2¼"h, 1¹⁵⁄₁₆"w, 2³⁄₁₆"d
Made for: Topps Co., Duryea, PA 18642
Made in: China
Cost new: $1.09 \ **Value:** $4.00 – 5.00
Description: Another in series of helmet containers. Embossed on the back: "™© 1995 Saban." Came with clear plastic wrap with ingredients written on it.

Power Ranger (head, Trini)

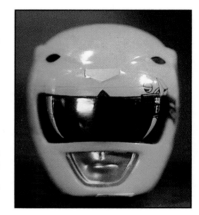

Category: Characters
Contents: Candy, 0.4 oz.
Size: 2¼"h, 1¹⁵⁄₁₆"w, 2³⁄₁₆"d
Made for: Topps Co., Duryea, PA 18642
Made in: China
Cost new: $1.09 \ **Value:** $4.00 – 5.00
Description: Another in the Power Rangers helmet container series. Embossed on the back: "™© 1995 Saban." Came with clear plastic wrap with ingredients written on it.

Power Ranger (head, Zack)

Category: Characters
Contents: Candy, 0.4 oz.
Size: 2¼"h, 1¹⁵⁄₁₆"w, 2⅛"d
Made for: Topps Co., Duryea, PA 18642
Made in: China
Cost new: $1.09 \ **Value:** $4.00 – 5.00
Description: Part of the Power Rangers helmet series. Embossed on the back: "™© 1995 Saban." Came with clear plastic wrap with ingredients written on it.

Presentation

Category: Miscellaneous
Contents: Caramels
Size: 4⅞"h, 4¾"w, 5½"d
Made for: Hershey Chocolate U.S.A., Hershey, PA 17033-0815
Value: $25.00 – 35.00
Description: A presentation container used by Hershey to promote new products for national distribution. Not sold to the public. Hershey's Classic Caramels is printed on the cover.

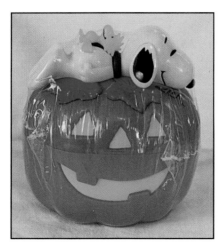

Pumpkin (Snoopy and Woodstock)

Category: Holidays
Contents: Whitman's candy, 3 oz.
Size: 4¹¹⁄₁₆"h, 4¼"w, 3⅝"d
Made for: Whitman's Candies, Kansas City, MO 64106
Made in: China
Cost new: $4.99 \ **Value:** $8.00 – 10.00
Description: Snoopy and Woodstock sleep on top of Halloween container. Has coin slot for use as a bank. Filled with Whitman's Candies. Embossed on the bottom: "Peanuts © United Feature Syndicate, Inc."

Pumpkin Head

Category: Holidays
Contents: Small colored beads
Size: 4³⁄₁₆"h, 1⅝"w, 1⅛"d
Made for: E. Rosen Company, Pawtucket, RI 02860
Value: $7.00 – 8.50
Description: This is an older version of Pumpkin Head (390726). The eyes and mouth are different, and also the tie. The head is the closure. Red and white paper tag on the back reads "Novelty and Candy Ing. Sugar, Corn Syrup, etc. E. Rosen Company, Pawtucket, RI 02860. Net Wt. ¾ oz." I can't find any other markings on container.

Pumpkin Head (390726)

Category: Holidays
Contents: Colored candy balls, ¾ oz.
Size: 4"h, 1⅝"w, 1⁵⁄₁₆"d
Made for: E. Rosen Co., Pawtucket, RI 02860
Made in: Hong Kong
Value: $5.00 – 7.00
Description: Pumpkin stands with right hand in pocket, left hand by his side. Head is the closure. Candy is black, white, yellow, and orange. #390726.

Pumpkin Head (wire)

Category: Holidays
Contents: Candy corn
Size: 2¾"h, 3⅛"w, 1⅝"d
Cost new: $0.98 \ **Value:** $2.00 – 3.00
Description: Measurements are head only. Has a string on top for hanging. Container has no markings. Plastic-covered wire arms and legs are poseable.

Pumpkin on a Stick

Category: Holidays
Contents: Colored beads
Size: 10"h, 1⁹⁄₁₆"w, 1⁵⁄₁₆"d
Made in: Hong Kong
Cost new: $0.27 \ **Value:** $5.00 – 6.00
Description: The paper tag reads "Duckwall – Alco $0.27."

Pumpkin Whistle

Category: Holidays
Contents: Small colored beads, ⅛ oz.
Size: 7¾"h, 1¾"w, ⁹⁄₁₆"d
Made for: E. Rosen Company, Pawtucket, RI 02860
Cost new: $0.19 \ **Value:** $8.00 – 10.00
Description: This is made in three pieces. You could take the middle (with candy) out and put the pumpkin head in the whistle and use it as a toy. The head is the closure. Red and white paper tag in the middle reads "Novelty and Candy Ing. Sugar, Corn Syrup, etc. E. Rosen Company, Pawtucket, RI 02860. #4 Net Wt. ¾ oz." I can't find any other markings on the container.

Push Pop

Category: Miscellaneous
Contents: Cherry candy, 0.6 oz.
Size: 3⅛"h, ¹⁵⁄₁₆"w, 1¹⁄₁₆"d
Made for: Topps Co., Duryea, PA 18642
Made in: Taiwan
Cost new: $0.49 \ **Value:** $1.00 – 2.50
Description: Embossed on top of the closure: "TOPPS." Has pocket clip. © 1985. Came in different colors and flavors.

Rabbit (361573)

Category: Animals
Contents: Round jelly beans, 1¼ oz.
Size: 5⅜"h, 1¾"w, 1⅜"d
Made for: E. Rosen Co., Pawtucket, RI 02860
Made in: China
Cost new: $0.69 \ **Value:** $5.00 – 7.00
Description: Container is similar to Mr. Rabbit, except detail is not as good, body not as clear. Embossed on the bottom: "made in China."

Rabbit (bank)

Category: Animals
Contents: Jelly beans, 3 oz.
Size: 4⁹⁄₁₆"h, 2⅝"w, 2⅝"d
Made for: Hilco Corp., Norristown, PA 19401
Made in: China
Value: $3.00 – 4.00
Description: Paper stick-ons for eyes and teeth. Slot on back of the head allows bank use. Embossed on the bottom: "© 1991 Hilco Corp. China 6."

Rabbit (Bendy Buddy Bunny)

Category: Animals
Contents: Gumballs, 0.52 oz.
Size: 3⅝"h, 1¹⁵⁄₁₆"w, 1⁹⁄₁₆"d (body)
Made for: Candy Containers & More Inc., Oxnard, CA 93030
Made in: China
Cost new: $0.95 \ **Value:** $2.00 – 3.00
Description: Has hole for a string between the ears. Blue eyes, pink nose. Arms and legs are flexible. Left ear tip bent down. Closure is push-in type on the back.

Rabbit (Bunny Bank)

Category: Gumball dispensers
Contents: Gum, 4 oz.
Size: 6¼"h, 3¾"w, 3½"d
Made for: Carousel Division Ford Gum & Machine Co., Inc., Akron, NY 14001
Made in: China
Cost new: $3.59 \ **Value:** $6.00 – 7.50
Description: Comes in a five-sided box. The front is open. Printed on the cap is "CAROUSEL." Embossed on the bottom is "Carousel, Made in China." Has a coin slot in the back, to be used as a bank. The box reads "Junior Bunny Gumball Machine Bank. Not recommended for children under age 3. Convenient slot for saving coins and dollar bills. Dispenses regular or sugarfree gumballs, candy, treats and more! It really works...just turn the handle to dispense gumball...no coins needed! Strong and break-resistant. Safe, non-toxic plastic."

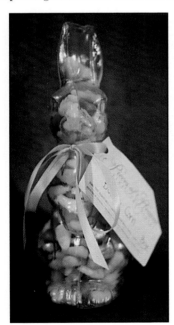

Rabbit (Bunny Corn)

Category: Animals
Contents: Candy corn, 8 oz.
Size: 8"h, 2¾"w, 3⅜"d
Made for: Pieces of Heaven, Carmel, CA 93923
Made in: West Germany
Value: $10.00 – 15.00
Description: Standing rabbit with hands together in front. Closure is on the bottom.

Rabbit (candy filled)

Category: Animals
Contents: Candy beads, ¾ oz.
Size: 4¹⁵⁄₁₆"h, 1⅝"w, 1¼"d
Made for: E. Rosen Company, Pawtucket, RI 02860
Made in: Hong Kong
Cost new: $0.47 \ **Value:** $6.00 – 8.00
Description: This is an older version of Mr. Rabbit. The head is the same, but he is standing on his own two feet. Mr. Rabbit is standing on a platform. Embossed on the bottom of his feet and the back of his head is "Hong Kong."

Rabbit (chrome)

→

Category: Animals
Contents: Chewy caramels, 3 oz.
Size: 3¾"h, 2⁹⁄₁₆"w, 3⅞"d
Made for: The Jelly Bean Factory, Fairfax, OH 45227
Made in: Taiwan
Cost new: $2.97 \ **Value:** $4.00 – 5.00
Description: Red ribbon tied to top ring. On bottom label, city is misspelled Fairax. Embossed on ring above the ears: "Made in Taiwan."

Rabbit (Cute & Cuddly)

←

Category: Animals
Contents: Colored candy, 0.99oz.
Size: 3⅛"h, 1¹³⁄₁₆"w, 1¹⁵⁄₁₆"d
Made for: R.L. Albert & Son, Inc., Greenwich, CT 06830
Made in: China
Cost new: $1.29 \ **Value:** $3.00 – 4.00
Description: This container has a clear plastic window in the stomach to view the candy. On the window is a sticker that reads "Cute & Cuddly." Closure is on the bottom. Container has a felt feel except for the closure.

Rabbit (Easter Unlimited)

→

Category: Animals
Contents: Jelly beans, ¾ oz.
Size: 2⅜"h, 2⅜"w, 3"d
Made for: E. Rosen Co., Pawtucket, RI 02860
Made in: China
Cost new: $0.95 \ **Value:** $3.00 – 5.00
Description: Embossed on bunny's left hip: "© Easterunlimtedinc."

Rabbit (Frankford)

←

Category: Animals
Contents: Hollow milk chocolate, 3 oz.
Size: 5¼"h, 2¾"w, 2⁹⁄₁₆"d
Made for: Frankford Candy & Chocolate Co., Philadelphia, PA 19146
Made in: Germany
Cost new: $1.97 \ **Value:** $3.00 – 4.00
Description: Can be used as a bank or an ornament. String can be tied through a hole in the head. Embossed in front between the legs: "Made in Germany."

Rabbit (Hilco)

Category: Gumball dispensers
Contents: Small candy balls
Size: 4"h, 2⅛"w, 1⅞"d
Made for: Hilco Corp., Norristown, PA 19401
Made in: China
Cost new: $0.99 \ **Value:** $2.00 – 3.50
Description: Sold at Easter time 2000. It has a metal chain and ring attached to the top. To get the candy you push the tab on the front and the candy comes out. Candy made in Canada. Net Wt. 1 oz. Can be used as a key chain. The label has dispense and refill instructions, nutrition facts, and ingredients.

Rabbit (holding egg)

Category: Animals
Contents: Chocolate, 1.75 oz.
Size: 4¾"h, 2½"w, 1⁷⁄₁₆"d
Made for: Frankford Candy & Chocolate Co., Philadelphia, PA 19146
Made in: Israel
Cost new: $1.50 \ **Value:** $2.50 – 3.00
Description: Has lope on the top for a string to be used as an ornament. Chocolate bunny is holding an Easter egg. The container is clear, but the bunny is pink, yellow, and blue. Has a coin slot in the back.

Rabbit (Jelly Eggs)

Category: Animals
Contents: Jelly Eggs, 2 oz.
Size: 5¹⁄₁₆"h, 1¹³⁄₁₆"w, 1¾"d
Made for: Lemberger Foods Co., Palisades Park, NJ
Made in: Hong Kong
Value: $7.50 – 10.00
Description: Eyes open and close as you move them. Eyelashes painted black.

Rabbit (Mr. Rabbit)

Category: Animals
Contents: Round jelly beans, 1¼ oz.
Size: 5½"h, 1¹³⁄₁₆"w, 1½"d
Made for: E. Rosen Co., Pawtucket, RI 02860
Made in: Hong Kong
Cost new: $0.59 \ **Value:** $5.00 – 7.50
Description: Right hand in his pocket, left hand by his side. Has jacket, tie, and belt. Ears, nose, and mouth are red. Eyes are black. Body nearly identical to Rabbit (361573).

Rabbit on Wheels

Category: Animals
Contents: Shaped like peanuts, 2 oz.
Size: 5¼"h, 2⁹⁄₁₆"w, 2½"d
Made for: E. Rosen Company, Providence, RI
Value: $20.00 – 30.00
Description: Made of clear plastic with a yellow tint. Has a string on the front of the wagon to pull it. Painted eyes, nose, and bow tie. The label on the bottom indicates E. Rosen was in Providence, Rhode Island, before moving to Pawtucket, Rhode Island.

Rain Sticks

Category: Miscellaneous
Contents: Gum, 0.88 oz.
Size: 11½"h, ¹⁵⁄₁₆"w
Made for: Cap Toys Inc., Bedford Heights, OH 44146
Made in: Mexico
Cost new: $0.99 \ **Value:** $2.50 – 3.00
Description: Paper label reads: "RAIN STICK gum. The Downpour That Sounds Delicious." © 1996.

Reindeer Barn

Category: Nonplastic
Contents: Chocolate, 2 oz.
Size: 3¼"h, 3"w, 1½"d
Made for: R.M. Palmer Co., West Reading, PA 19611
Cost new: $0.79 \ **Value:** $2.00 – 3.00
Description: This container is made of paper. It has a punch out spot on the roof to put a string in to be used as a Christmas ornament. There are others in this series.

RE-USE-IT

Category: Miscellaneous
Contents: Gum, 2 oz.
Size: 1¾"h, 2½"w, 2³⁄₁₆"d
Made for: Leaf Inc., Lake Forest, IL 60045
Made in: Canada
Cost new: $0.49 \ **Value:** $2.00 – 3.00
Description: Doubles as container for used gum. Label reads "Rain-Blo brand, RE-USE-IT." Embossed on the bottom: "MFTG IN CANADA."

Riddler (bust)

Category: Characters
Contents: Gum, 0.4 oz.
Size: 2½"h, 2³⁄₁₆"w, 1⅜"d
Made for: Topps Co., Duryea, PA 18642
Made in: China
Cost new: $0.97 \ **Value:** $3.50 – 5.50
Description: The Riddler of Batman fame. Embossed on the back: "™& © DC COMICS 1995."

Roadside Diner (Coke)

Category: Nonplastic
Contents: English toffee, 8 oz.
Size: 4"h, 8½"w, 2⅝"d
Made for: Golden Harvest Products, Inc., Overland Park, KS 66203
Cost new: $9.95 \ **Value:** $12.00 – 15.00
Description: Container is made out of tin. Has a sticker that reads "Authorized Coca-Cola Product 1940, Coca-Cola Diner Series I." Comes sealed in plastic wrap.

Robot

Category: Characters
Contents: Gum
Size: 3¾"h, 2½"w, 1⅛"d
Made in: Hong Kong
Value: $20.00 – 25.00
Description: Arms and legs move. Embossed on the back: "Made in Hong Kong."

Robot (Marty Moon Man)

Category: Characters
Contents: Candy
Size: 3¹⁄₁₆"h, 1⅜"w, ⁹⁄₁₆"d
Made for: R.L. Albert & Son, Inc., New York, NY 10457
Made in: Hong Kong
Value: $12.00 – 15.00
Description: The arms and propeller move. The head comes off to open the container. Net Wt. 0.10 oz.

Rock →

Category: Miscellaneous
Contents: Gum, 0.88 oz.
Size: 1⅝"h, 2"w, 1"d
Made for: Goodlite Products Inc., Bedford, TX 76021
Made in: China
Cost new: $0.69 \ Value: $3.00 – 4.00
Description: Has "ROCK" embossed on the front. Item No. FT20303. Screw-on closure. Came with a carrying cord.

← Rocket (Arturito)

Category: Transportation
Contents: Liquid candy
Size: 3⅛"h, 1⅝"w
Made for: New Invention Confectionary Mexico
Made in: Mexico
Cost new: $0.50 \ Value: $2.00 – 3.50
Description: Has a rocket on the side of the container. Has 18 small holes on top to squeeze out the candy.

Rocket (Astro Blaster) →

Category: Games
Contents: Colored candy balls
Size: 8⅛"h, 1¹¹⁄₁₆"w
Made for: Bee International, Chula Vista, CA 91912
Made in: China
Value: $2.50 – 4.00
Description: This container shoots a foam rubber rocket. Embossed on the inside plunger is "Made in China."

← Rocket (Star Ship)

Category: Transportation
Contents: Candy, 28 gr
Size: 3⅝"h, 1⅞"w
Made for: De Jongh
Made in: Mexico
Cost new: $0.50 \ Value: $3.00 – 4.00
Description: Has a paper label that reads "STAR SHIP – movies candy – space gel candy – This toy is not suitable for children under 5. Made in Mexico for De Jongh, S.A. Avda. DIAGONAL, 662 08034 BARCELONA, SPAIN. Registered Trademark Models and Designs, all rights reserved, © XCVI-E BERNATE F.S.A." The label on this container is written in English and Spanish.

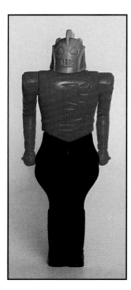

Rocketeer (full body)

Category: Characters
Contents: Gum, 0.3 oz.
Size: 5¼"h, 2"w, 1⅛"d
Made for: The Topps Co., Duryea, PA 18642
Made in: Taiwan
Value: $3.50 – 5.00
Description: From the Disney movie. Remove head to get candy. The arms move and the backpack is removable.

Rocketeer (head)

Category: Characters
Contents: Candy, 0.4 oz.
Size: 2½"h, 1½"w, 2⅝"d
Made for: Topps Co., Duryea, PA 18642
Made in: China
Cost new: $0.69 \ **Value:** $3.50 – 5.00
Description: From the Disney movie "The Rocketeer." Helmet only. Embossed on the bottom: "© DISNEY."

Rocketeer (waist up)

Category: Characters
Contents: Candy, 0.15 oz.
Size: 2½"h, 1⅝"w, 1"d
Made for: Topps Co., Duryea, PA 18642
Made in: China
Cost new: $0.69 \ **Value:** $3.50 – 5.00
Description: From the Disney movie. Head moves, closure on the bottom. Also embossed there: "© DISNEY."

Rocking Horse

Category: Animals
Contents: Tart 'N' Tangy, 3 oz.
Size: 3⅝"h, 4"w, 1⁹⁄₁₆"d
Made for: The Jelly Bean Factory, Fairfax, OH 45227
Made in: Germany
Cost new: $1.25 \ **Value:** $4.50 – 5.50
Description: Has ring on back of the neck with a red bow. Can be used as a Christmas ornament. Label is under the rocker.

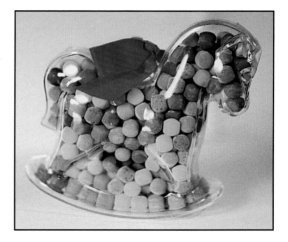

Rocking Horse (bank)

Category: Animals
Contents: Candy, 2.25 oz.
Size: 5⅞"h, 5⅝"w, 1³⁄₁₆"d
Made for: Candy Containers & More Inc., Oxnard, CA 93030
Made in: China
Cost new: $1.99 \ **Value:** $4.50 – 5.50
Description: Paper label on the bottom of the container. Clear plastic window shows candy inside container. Has a coin slot on top with a sticker covering the slot. Front and back are made the same.

Roller Blade (whistle)

Category: Transportation
Contents: Small candy beads
Size: 2⅞"h, 1"w, 3⁷⁄₁₆"d
Cost new: $0.25 \ **Value:** $6.00 – 8.00
Description: Has a carrying cord. Screw-top closure. Wheels do not move. No markings. Purchased in Yuma, Arizona, in 1995.

Roller Blades

Category: Transportation
Contents: Pressed colored candy, 0.3 oz.
Size: 3⅛"h, 1"w, 2⅝"d
Made for: Topps Co., Duryea, PA 18642
Made in: China
Value: $7.50 – 9.50
Description: All four wheels turn. Has a stand by last wheel. © 1991.

Roller Pop

Category: Miscellaneous
Contents: Powdered candy
Size: 4½"h, 3⅝"w, ¾"d
Made for: Topps Co., Duryea, PA 18642
Made in: Thailand
Cost new: $0.89 \ **Value:** $2.00 – 3.50
Description: Package came with paint pan, roller, and pack of powder candy. Came in many colors. Front of the package reads "New! ROLLER POP CANDY. Candy N' Powder that Paints your Mouth!" Flavors: grape, strawberry, cherry, and lemon-lime. © 1994.

Roller Skates

Category: Transportation
Contents: Pressed colored candy, 0.4 oz.
Size: 2¼"h, 1¼"w, 2¾"d
Made for: Topps Co., Duryea, PA 18642
Made in: China
Cost new: $0.69 \ **Value:** $5.00 – 8.00
Description: Has a plastic string attached to back of the shoe. Push closure. © 1991.

Ronald (McDonald's)

Category: Characters
Contents: Nerds
Size: 2⅞"h, 2¼"w, 1⅝"d
Made for: McDonald's Corp., Oak Brook, IL 60521
Made in: China
Cost new: free w/Happy Meal \ **Value:** $1.00 – 2.00
Description: Marketed as McDonald's Happy Meal toy. One of a series of six. This one is #5. Plastic wrap has messages in English, French, and Spanish. It comes with a separate bag of Wonka Spooky Nerds candy. You can lift the mask on the container to see the character and put the candy in. The mask is the closure. Also there is a spring loaded door on the bottom. Embossed on the back of the container is "© 1998 McDonald's Corp. China/Chine WI 19."

Santa (361520)

Category: Holidays
Contents: Round jelly beans, 1¼ oz.
Size: 4¼"h, 1¹³⁄₁₆"w, 1½"d
Made for: E. Rosen Co., Pawtucket, RI 02860
Made in: Hong Kong
Cost new: $0.40 \ **Value:** $6.00 – 8.00
Description: Paper label reads "Candy Filled Santa. SANTA 361520." Only head is painted, the rest of the body is clear. Standing on a platform. Embossed on back of the cap: "Hong Kong."

Santa (eating from tin)

Category: Nonplastic
Contents: Raspberry-flavored candies, 50g
Size: ¹⁵⁄₁₆"h, 2¹⁵⁄₁₆"w
Made for: S.A. La Vosgienne, France
Made in: France
Cost new: $1.50 \ **Value:** $2.50 – 3.50
Description: Has Santa eating candy from a tin with buildings in the background. Container made of tin.

Santa (Flix)

Category: Gumball dispensers
Contents: Gumball, 0.54 oz.
Size: 5³⁄₁₆"h, 1⅝"w, 1¹¹⁄₁₆"d
Made for: Imagining 3, Niles, IL 60714
Made in: China
Cost new: $2.75 \ **Value:** $4.00 – 6.00
Description: Gumball machine. Has "Flix" embossed on the front, and
"patents pending – 5,385,267, D358, 232 Made in China," on the bottom.

Santa (jumping)

Category: Holidays
Contents: Colored candy balls
Size: 5"h, 1½"w
Made in: China
Value: $8.00 – 10.00
Description: This container is also an action toy. When you push it down, the suction
cup sticks to a smooth surface for a short time. Then it springs up. Embossed on the
bottom is "MADE IN CHINA." The head is the closure. A snowman is made the same.

Santa (large bendy)

Category: Holidays
Contents: Gum, 1.74 oz.
Size: 4¹⁄₁₆"h, 2⅞"w, 2"d
Made for: Candy Containers & More Inc., Oxnard, CA 93030
Made in: China
Cost new: $1.25 \ **Value:** $2.50 – 3.00
Description: Push-in closure on the back. Ring on top for hanging.
Santa is giving two thumbs up. Arms and legs are poseable. Only
hat, eyes, and mustache are painted. Body is clear.

Santa Candy Dish

Category: Holidays
Contents: Hershey's Kisses, 4 oz.
Size: Boxed 8⅜"h, 4⅛"w, 4¾"d
Made for: Hershey Chocolate U.S.A., Hershey, PA 17033-0815
Made in: China
Value: $5.00 – 7.50
Description: Santa is holding his bag, which is filled with candy.
Box made to look like sleigh with Santa riding in it. Santa's cap
removes for easy filling. © 1994.

Santa Claus (angle hat)

Category: Holidays
Contents: Small colored beads, ¾ oz.
Size: 4"h, 1¹³⁄₁₆"w, 1½"d
Made for: E. Rosen Company, Pawtucket, RI 02860
Made in: Hong Kong
Value: $6.00 – 8.00
Description: The head is the closure. Red and white paper tag on the back reads "Novelty and Candy Ing. Sugar, Corn Syrup, etc. E. Rosen Company, Pawtucket, RI 02860. Net Wt.¾ oz." I can't find any other markings on container.

Santa Claus (head)

Category: Holidays
Contents: Small pack of candy beads & holiday stickers
Size: 2⁷⁄₁₆"h, 2³⁄₈"w, 2¹⁄₁₆"d
Made in: China
Cost new: $0.49 \ **Value:** $3.50 – 4.00
Description: Closure is on the bottom, embossed with "Made in China." Container can be hung as an ornament. Inside are small package of candy and two peel-off stickers. Santa's eyes are closed.

Santa Claus (round head)

Category: Holidays
Contents: Gumballs
Size: 6"h, 1⅝"w, 1⅞"d
Made for: Hilco Corp., Norristown, PA 19401
Made in: China
Cost new: $1.00 \ **Value:** $3.00 – 4.50
Description: Red top and bottom. Clear middle with paper picture of Santa from waist up. Embossed on the bottom: "HILCO corporation 1992 Made in China."

Santa Claus (wire)

Category: Holidays
Contents: Jelly beans, 2 oz.
Size: 3⅛"h, 2¹⁄₁₆"w, 1¾"d (body)
Made for: Horizon Candy, El Paso, TX 79906
Made in: China
Cost new: $1.00 \ **Value:** $2.00 – 3.00
Description: Moveable plastic-covered arms and legs. Only hat, eyes, and mustache are painted. Body is clear.

Screw Ups

Category: Battery operated
Contents: Tart 'N' Tinys, 1.6 oz.
Size: 4⅝"h, 3"w, 1"d
Made for: Cap Toys Inc., Bedford Hts, OH 44146
Made in: China
Value: $3.50 – 5.50
Description: Label reads "The Candy Gadget with a Colorful Twist." Takes AAA battery.

Screw-Bot

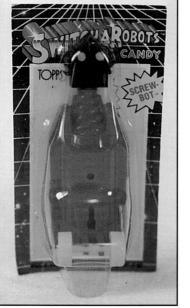

Category: Transportation
Contents: Candy, 0.2 oz.
Size: 3½"h, 1¼"w, 1⁹⁄₁₆"d
Made for: Topps Chewing Gum Inc., Duryea, PA 18642
Made in: Hong Kong
Value: $7.50 – 10.00
Description: Series of transforming robot containers: Screw-Bot, Bat-Bot, and Blast-Bot. Label says "Switcharobots come to earth with a mission TO BRING YOU CANDY!" © 1986.

Shark

Category: Animals
Contents: Colored candy beads
Size: 1⅞"h, 2"w, 5⅞"d
Made for: Allen Mitchell Products, Oxnard, CA 93030
Made in: Hong Kong
Value: $6.50 – 9.00
Description: The shark's mouth opens and closes when you press the lever on top. The top fin has a hole in it so you can hang it as an ornament.

Ship (Friend Ship)

Category: Transportation
Contents: Conversation hearts, 3 oz.
Size: 1¹³⁄₁₆"h, 3"w, 6¾"d
Made for: E.J. Brach & Sons Inc., Chicago, IL 60644
Value: $4.50 – 5.50
Description: The smoke stacks and port holes are shaped like hearts. Cardboard insert has a heart with an anchor through it. It also reads "BRACH*S® Friend Ship 360-556."

Ship (war)

Category: Transportation
Contents: Small candy balls
Size: ½"h, ½"w, 3¼"d
Made in: West Germany
Value: $7.50 – 10.00
Description: Ship with guns facing front and back.

Shoe (Jammin' Jumpers)

Category: Miscellaneous
Contents: Candy socks, 0.3 oz.
Size: 2³⁄₁₆"h, 1⁵⁄₁₆"w, 3"d
Made for: The Topps Co., Duryea, PA 18642
Made in: China
Value: $5.00 – 7.50
Description: Comes in blue, white, orange, and black with different colored laces and soles. The candy inside is shaped like socks. Embossed on the sole: "© 1990 The Topps Co. Inc."

Shoe (Yo Landa!)

Category: Miscellaneous
Contents: Candy shaped like shoes, 0.3 oz.
Size: 2⅛"h, 1¼"w, 3"d
Made for: The Topps Co., Duryea, PA 18642
Made in: China
Value: $5.00 – 7.50
Description: Closer is a push in. Embossed on the sole: "© 1990 The Topps Co. Inc. Yo Stupid." There are three in the series, Yo Stupid!, Yo Slick!, and Yo Landa!

Shoe (Yo Slick!)

Category: Miscellaneous
Contents: Candy shaped like shoes, 0.3 oz.
Size: 1¹⁵⁄₁₆"h, 1⁵⁄₁₆"w, 2⅞"d
Made for: The Topps Co., Duryea, PA 18642
Made in: China
Value: $5.00 – 7.50
Description: Closer is a push in. Embossed on the sole: "© 1990 The Topps Co. Inc. Yo Stupid." There are three in the series, Yo Stupid!, Yo Slick!, and Yo Landa!

Shoe (Yo Stupid!)

Category: Miscellaneous
Contents: Candy shaped like shoes, 0.3 oz.
Size: 2⅛"h, 1⁷⁄₁₆"w, 3"d
Made for: The Topps Co., Duryea, PA 18642
Made in: China
Value: $5.00 – 7.50
Description: Closer is a push in. Embossed on the sole: "© 1990 The Topps Co. Inc. Yo Stupid." There are three in the series, Yo Stupid!, Yo Slick!, and Yo Landa!

Skittles (power)

Category: Battery operated
Contents: Skittles candy, 1.41 oz.
Size: 4"h, 3⅝"w, 1⅜"d
Made for: Cap Toys Inc., Bedford Hts., OH 44146
Made in: China
Cost new: $4.49 \ **Value:** $5.00 – 6.00
Description: Comes on a card with a pack of candy. Paper sticker on the front of the container reads "Power Skittles Taste the Rainbow." NO.4755. Has a belt clip.

Skull (Scary Skulls)

Category: Miscellaneous
Contents: Bubble gumballs
Size: 3⅝"h, 2¼"w, 2⅝"d
Made for: Frankford Candy & Chocolate Co., Philadelphia, PA 19146
Made in: China
Cost new: $1.00 \ **Value:** $3.00 – 4.00
Description: Comes with a plastic cord and is made to be a necklace. The paper tag reads "Scary Skulls, Halloween Necklace filled with Bubble Gum Balls!" The eyes, nose, and mouth are painted white.

Slappy's Candy Keeper

Category: Characters
Contents: Medium-sized candy balls
Size: 3⅝"h, 2¼"w, 2⅛"d
Made for: Taco Bell Corp.
Made in: China
Cost new: free w/Happy Meal \ **Value:** $2.00 – 3.00
Description: Taco Bell featured Goosebumps toy. Series of four: Slappy, Skull Mobile, Cuddles the Horrible Hamster, and Wrappin' Mummy. Bottom embossed with: "™ & © Parachute Press, Inc. Mfg. by Strottman."

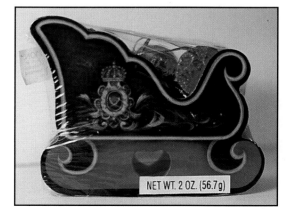

Sleigh

Category: Nonplastic
Contents: Milk chocolate, 2 oz.
Size: 3⅝"h, 4⅜"w, 1⅝"d
Made for: Frankford Candy & Chocolate Co., Philadelphia, PA 19146
Value: $4.50 – 5.50
Description: Made out of wood. Sleigh holds bell-shaped candy. Tag on the back reads "CAUTION: The sleigh is an ornament, not a toy. Not recommended for children."

Sleigh (Snoopy and Woodstock)

Category: Holidays
Contents: Chocolates, 3 oz.
Size: 5"h, 2⁹⁄₁₆"w, 4⁷⁄₈"d
Made for: Whitman's Candies, Kansas City, Missouri 64106
Made in: China
Cost new: $4.99 \ **Value:** $7.00 – 8.50
Description: Coin slot in toy bag. Season's Greetings on the right side. Embossed on the bottom, under the label: "PEANUTS © Feature Syndicate, Inc. Made in China."

Snake

Category: Animals
Contents: Candy beads, 20g
Size: ¾"h, 1¹⁄₁₆"w, 8¾"l
Made for: Imperial Toy Corporation, Los Angeles, CA 90021
Made in: China
Cost new: $1.59 \ **Value:** $4.00 – 6.00
Description: Called Candy Rattle Snake. Shake the snake and you can hear it rattle. The head is the closure. Filled with Sconza Fruit Spots. Made of hard plastic. The candy is black and green.

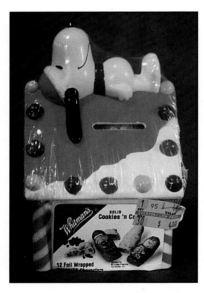

Snoopy (on dog house)

Category: Characters
Contents: Individually wrapped Cookies 'n Cream, 3 oz.
Size: 6¼"h, 3⅝"w, 3¹⁵⁄₁₆"d
Made for: Whitman's Candies, Kansas City, MO 64106
Made in: China
Cost new: $4.99 \ **Value:** $6.00 – 8.00
Description: Snoopy and Woodstock laying on top of dog house. A Christmas scene with snow on roof, colored balls, and candy-striped corner posts. Snoopy's name over the door and Whitman's Candies on the back. Embossed on the bottom: "Peanuts © United Feature Syndicate, Inc. Made in China."

Snoopy and Woodstock (egg, flat bottom)

Category: Characters
Contents: Milk chocolate, 3 oz.
Size: 4⅞"h, 4⅜"w, 3¼"d
Made for: Whitman's Candies, Kansas City, MO 64106
Made in: China
Cost new: $4.47 \ **Value:** $6.00 – 8.00
Description: Snoopy and Woodstock laying on an Easter egg. Also a bank. Filled with 12 foil-wrapped Peanuts characters. This 1998 egg has a flat bottom. Egg from 1997 had a round bottom. Embossed on the bottom: "Peanuts © United Feature Syndicate, Inc. Made in China."

Snoopy and Woodstock (on egg)

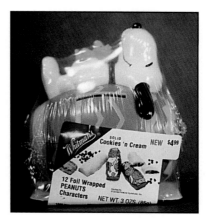

Category: Characters
Contents: Cookies 'n Cream, 3 oz.
Size: 5"h, 4⅜"w, 3¼"d
Made for: Whitman's Candies, Kansas City, MO 64106
Made in: China
Cost new: $4.99 \ **Value:** $6.00 – 8.00
Description: Snoopy and Woodstock laying on an Easter egg. Also a bank. Filled with 12 foil-wrapped Peanuts characters. 1997. Comes glued to a piece of cardboard.

Snoopy Halloween House

Category: Characters
Contents: Milk chocolate, 3 oz.
Size: 6½"h, 3½"w, 4"d
Made for: Whitman's Candies, Kansas City, MO 64106
Made in: China
Cost new: $3.99 \ **Value:** $6.00 – 8.00
Description: Snoopy is laying on his dog house. Snoopy has yellow teeth and a black cape for Halloween. The house has a green fingers hanging out the coin slot. It is filled with 12 foil wrapped solid milk chocolate Peanuts® characters. Embossed on the bottom: "Peanuts © United Feature Syndicate Inc. Made in China 04."

Snow Man (Blow Mold Small)

Category: Holidays
Contents: Tart 'N' Tangy, 3.25 oz.
Size: 4⅜"h, 2⁹⁄₁₆"w, 2⅛"d
Made for: Dayton Hudson Corp., Minneapolis, MN 55402
Made in: Mexico
Cost new: $0.99 \ **Value:** $3.50 – 4.50
Description: Has cloth plaid scarf. Label on bottom reads "DPCI:055030020 Blow Mold Snowman Small w/Tart'N Tangy Candy." Ingredients label on back.

Snow Man (Flix)

Category: Gumball dispensers
Contents: Gumballs, 0.54 oz.
Size: 5⁹⁄₁₆"h, 1⅝"w, 1¾"d
Made for: Imaginings 3, Niles, IL 60714
Made in: China
Cost new: $2.75 \ **Value:** $4.00 – 5.00
Description: Gumball machine. Has "Flix" embossed on the front, and "patents pending – 5,385,267, D358, 232 Made in China," on the bottom.

Snow Man (jumping)

Category: Holidays
Size: 5"h, 1½"w
Made in: China
Value: $6.00 – 8.00
Description: This container is also an action toy. When you push it down, the suction cup sticks to a smooth surface for a short time. Then it springs up. Embossed on the bottom is "MADE IN CHINA." The head is the closure. A Santa is made the same.

Snow Man (top hat and cane)

Category: Characters
Contents: Small colored beads
Size: 4⅝"h, 1¾"w, 1⁹⁄₁₆"d
Made in: Hong Kong
Value: $7.00 – 8.50
Description: Embossed on the back of the head and back: "Hong Kong." He is wearing a scarf, has two buttons, and is holding a cane.

Snowman (head)

Category: Characters
Contents: Small colored balls & holiday stickers
Size: 2⅝"h, 2½"w, 2¼"d
Made in: China
Value: $3.50 – 4.50
Description: Closure on the bottom, embossed with "Made In China." Has place on top for hanging as an ornament. Inside are small package of candy and two peel-off stickers. Snowman has ear muffs and knit cap. Head only.

Snowman (See's)

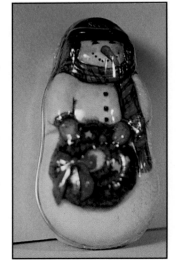

Category: Nonplastic
Contents: Candy, 2 oz.
Size: 4¼"h, 2¼"w, 1⅞"d
Made for: See's Candy Shop Inc., Los Angeles, CA
Made in: China
Value: $2.50 – 4.00
Description: Has a string on top to be used as an ornament. Made of tin. © 1994.

Soccer (gumball machine)

Category: Gumball dispensers
Contents: Gumballs, 1.1 oz.
Size: 4"h, 2⅜"w, 2¹¹⁄₁₆"d
Made for: Candy Containers & More Inc., Oxnard, CA 93030
Made in: China
Cost new: $0.95 \ **Value:** $2.00 – 3.00
Description: Comes in different colors. Turn handle on the front to get gumballs. Under paper label is embossed: "PATENT PENDING MADE IN CHINA."

Soccer Ball (gum machine)

Category: Gumball dispensers
Contents: Gum, 2.0 oz.
Size: 3¾"h, 2¼"w
Made for: Bee International, Chula Vista, CA 91912
Made in: China
Cost new: $0.99 \ **Value:** $2.00 – 3.00
Description: Embossed on the bottom: "© 1997 C. L. MADE IN CHINA." Embossed on the front are three bees. Turn the handle and the gum comes out. It is also made with a basketball, baseball, and football.

Soccer Power Sours

Category: Miscellaneous
Contents: Sours candy, 1 oz.
Size: ⅞"h, 2½"w
Made for: BerZerk Candy Werks, Memphis, TN 38119
Cost new: $0.50 \ **Value:** $1.00 – 2.00
Description: Candy inside shaped like soccer balls.

Soldier

Category: Characters
Contents: Gumballs
Size: 6"h, 1⅝"w, 1⅞"d
Made for: Hilco Corp., Norristown, PA 19401
Made in: China
Cost new: $1.00 \ **Value:** $3.00 – 4.50
Description: Black top and bottom. Clear middle with paper picture of a soldier. Embossed on the bottom: "HILCO corporation © 1992. Made in China."

Soldier (milk chocolate)

Category: Characters
Contents: Milk chocolate, 2.5 oz.
Size: 5⁹⁄₁₆"h, 2½"w, 2⅛"d
Made for: Frankford Candy & Chocolate Co., Philadelphia, PA 19146
Made in: China
Value: $2.00 – 3.00
Description: Clear container with milk chocolate soldier inside. Brown with white belts and red shoulder and hat decorations. Has hanging ring on top. Label reads "Frankford Traditions Deluxe. Hollow Milk Chocolate." Inside card: "Easy to open, Refillable, Ornament, Great Stocking Stuffer."

Sonic

Category: Characters
Contents: Gum, 0.4 oz.
Size: 3⅝"h, 2⅜"w, 2⅜"d
Made for: The Topps Co., Duryea, PA 18642
Made in: China
Value: $14.00 – 18.00
Description: Embossed on the under side of the left foot: "© 1993 SEGA." Inside is multi-colored pebble-shaped gum.

Sonic Game Gear

Category: Miscellaneous
Contents: Gum, 1.05 oz.
Size: ¾"h, 4⅝"w, 2½"d
Made for: Amurol Confections Co., Yorkville IL 60560
Made in: U.S.A.
Cost new: $1.09 \ **Value:** $3.00 – 4.50
Description: Came with Sonic the Hedgehog trading cards. Game Gear™, Sega™. © 1994.

Spider (brown)

Category: Animals
Contents: Candy beads in a package
Size: ⅞"h, 3¾"w, 3¼"d
Made in: Hong Kong
Value: $3.50 – 5.00
Description: Soft plastic. Has pack of candy hidden in hind end.

Spider (on cup)

Category: Animals
Contents: Pressed colored pellets, 0.3 oz.
Size: 1⅞"h, 3½"w, 2¼"d
Made for: Topps Co., Duryea, PA 18642
Made in: China
Cost new: $0.49 \ **Value:** $4.00 – 5.00
Description: Has a suction cup on the bottom. Yellow eyes and red-tipped pincer. © 1990.

Spin Pop (Dolly Lolly)

Category: Battery operated
Contents: Lollipop, 0.6 oz.
Size: 9"h, 1¼"w, 1"d
Made for: Cap Toys Inc., Bedford Heights, OH 44146
Made in: China
Cost new: $2.99 \ **Value:** $4.00 – 5.00
Description: Takes AA battery. Button on right side makes doll turn around. Lollipop comes out of her head. Label reads "Dolly Lolly Spin Pop." No. 4510, U.S. Patent No. 5,209. © 1995.

Spin Pop (Easter)

Category: Battery operated
Contents: Lollipop, 0.6 oz.
Size: 8¾"h, 1⅞"w, 1¾"d
Made for: Cap Toys Inc., Bedford Heights, OH 44146
Made in: China
Cost new: $2.99 \ **Value:** $4.00 – 5.00
Description: Battery makes ears spin. Rabbit is sitting with basket of Easter eggs in his lap. Ears are twisted around. Label reads "Press Here – Easter Spin Pop Candy." No. 4065; U.S. Patent No. 5,209,692. © 1996.

Spin Pop (Marvin)

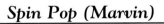

Category: Battery operated
Contents: Lollipop
Size: 6⅞"h, 1⁹⁄₁₆"w, 2¾"d
Made for: Cap Toys Inc., Bedford Heights, OH 44146
Made in: China
Cost new: $2.99 \ **Value:** $4.00 – 5.00
Description: Press the button and the sucker turns and Marvin's arm goes up and down. Looney Toons. No. 4525.

Splashers

Category: Nonplastic
Contents: Bubble gum, 2 oz.
Size: 2"h, 2⅝"w
Made for: Concord Confections Inc., Ontario, Canada
Made in: Canada
Value: $2.00 – 2.50
Description: Made out of tin. Looks like a small paint can. Paper label reads "Tongue Splashers Bubble Gum. Assorted colors & flavors. Paints your mouth with a splash of color!"

Sport Pal (golf ball)

Category: Characters
Contents: Gum, 2 oz.
Size: 3"h, 2¾"w, 2¾"d
Made for: The Jelly Bean Factory, Fairfax, OH 45227
Made in: China
Cost new: $1.97 \ **Value:** $3.00 – 4.00
Description: Has tab with hole for hanging. Arms and legs are poseable. Other containers are baseball and soccer ball.

Sports Bottle

Category: Bottles and jars
Contents: Liquid candy, 4 oz.
Size: 5"h, 1¹³⁄₁₆"w
Made for: Amurol Products Co., Naperville, IL 60566
Made in: U.S.A.
Value: $3.00 – 4.50
Description: Came in three flavors: Red-Cherry, Green-Watermelon, Blue-Blue Raspberry. © 1992.

Squirrel #2

Category: Animals
Contents: Red candy, ⅝ oz.
Size: 3⅜"h, 2¼"w, 1"d
Made for: Leader Candies Inc., Brooklyn, NY
Made in: Hong Kong
Value: $7.00 – 10.00
Description: Embossed on the back of the #2 is "HONG KONG." The head moves and is the closure. On the end of the 2 is a tail. There are three round bumps that I assume are his paws. Has a paper label on the backside.

Statue of Liberty

Category: Miscellaneous
Contents: Gum, 0.4 oz.
Size: 4¹³⁄₁₆"h, 1¾"w, 1⅛"d
Made for: Topps Chewing Gum Inc., Duryea, PA 18642
Made in: Hong Kong
Value: $11.00 – 15.00
Description: Label reads: "© 1986 Topps Chewing Gum Inc." It also comes in blue and white.

Stinky

Category: Characters
Contents: Bubble gum, 0.4 oz.
Size: 2⅛"h, 2¼"w, 2"d
Made for: Topps Co., Duryea, PA 18642
Made in: China
Cost new: $1.29 \ **Value:** $3.00 – 4.00
Description: Stinky is one of Casper's friends. Glows in the dark. Head only, with yellow eyes and black eyebrows. Embossed on the back: "Casper © 1995 UCS and Amblin. ™Harvey."

Storm Trooper (head)

Category: Characters
Contents: Colored candy pellets, 0.7 oz.
Size: 2½"h, 1¹¹⁄₁₆"w, 1⅝"d
Made for: Topps Co., Duryea, PA 18642
Made in: Hong Kong
Value: $4.50 – 6.50
Description: Embossed on the closure: "Star Wars The Empire Strikes Back." To get the candy out, turn closure to hole in the container. © 1980.

Strawberry

Category: Food items
Contents: Powdered candy, ⅝ oz.
Size: 2⅞"h, 1¾"w, 1½"d
Made for: Ce De Candy Inc., Union, NJ 07083
Made in: U.S.A.
Cost new: $0.40 \ **Value:** $1.50 – 3.00
Description: Screw cap has a ring for hanging. Paper label under the cap.

Stretch

Category: Characters
Contents: Bubble gum, 0.4 oz.
Size: 2⁹⁄₁₆"h, 1⁹⁄₁₆"w, 2³⁄₁₆"d
Made for: The Topps Co., Duryea, PA 18642
Made in: China
Cost new: $1.29 \ **Value:** $3.00 – 4.00
Description: Stretch is one of Casper's friends. Glows in the dark. Head only, with violet eyes and black eyebrows. Embossed on the back: "Casper © 1995 UCS and Amblin. ™Harvey."

Super Gumputer

Category: Battery operated
Contents: Bubble gum, 2 oz.
Size: 4⅝"h, 2¹³⁄₁₆"w, 1⁵⁄₁₆"d
Made for: Amurol Confections Co., Yorkville, IL 60560
Made in: China
Cost new: $1.29 \ **Value:** $3.00 – 5.00
Description: Label on the back reads "Made In U.S.A.," but bottom embossed with "Made In China." Features three different colors of bubble gum: fruit, watermelon, and grape.

Surprise Tin (Batman)

Category: Nonplastic
Contents: Milk chocolate marshmallow, ⅞ oz.
Size: 4"h, 2¹³⁄₁₆"w, 1⅞"d
Made for: Whitman's Candies, Kansas City, MO 64106
Made in: China
Cost new: $1.97 \ **Value:** $3.00 – 4.00
Description: Tin contains candy, character figure, and stickers. Part of a series featuring cartoon characters. © 1997.

Surprise Tin (Batman and Robin)

Category: Nonplastic
Contents: Chocolate-covered marshmallow bar, ⅞ oz.
Size: 4"h, 2¹³⁄₁₆"w, 1⅞"d
Made for: Whitman's Candies Inc., Kansas City, MO 64106
Made in: China
Cost new: $1.97 \ **Value:** $3.00 – 4.00
Description: Has candy, character figure, and stickers inside. Made of tin. Side reads "MC Covered Marshmallow Bar + Surprise + Stickers. Batman and all related characters, names, and indicia are trademarks of DC Comics. © 1997 Copyright © Whitman's Candy Inc." Part of a series of five.

Surprise Tin (Snoopy running)

Category: Nonplastic
Contents: Chocolate-covered marshmallows, ⅞ oz.
Size: 4"h, 2¹³⁄₁₆"w, 1⅞"d
Made for: Whitman's Candies, Kansas City, MO 64106
Made in: China
Cost new: $1.97 \ **Value:** $3.00 – 4.00
Description: Has candy, character figure, and stickers inside. Made of tin. Side reads "Chocolate Covered Marshmallow + Surprise Toy + Stickers. Copyright © Whitman's Candy Inc." Part of a series of five characters.

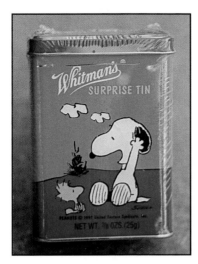

Surprise Tin (Snoopy sitting)

Category: Nonplastic
Contents: Chocolate-covered marshmallow, ⅞ oz.
Size: 4"h, 2¹³⁄₁₆"w, 1⅞"d
Made for: Whitman's Candies, Kansas City, MO 64106
Made in: China
Cost new: $1.97 \ **Value:** $3.00 – 4.00
Description: Part of a series of surprise tins. Has candy, character figure, and stickers inside. Side reads "Chocolate Covered Marshmallow & Surprise Toy & Stickers. Copyright © Whitman's Candy Inc."

Sword (Pegasus)

Category: Characters
Contents: Sweet Tarts, 2.5 oz.
Size: 14⅜"h, 3¹⁄₁₆"w, 2¹¹⁄₁₆"d
Made for: Nestle, St. Louis, MO 63125
Made in: China
Value: $7.50 – 10.00
Description: From Disney's "Hercules." Embossed on hilt: "© Disney."

TV

Category: Miscellaneous
Contents: Gum
Size: 1¼"h, 1¾"w, ¹³⁄₁₆"d
Made in: China
Cost new: $0.25 \ **Value:** $2.50 – 3.00
Description: Made to look like a TV. Has a paper sticker for the picture tube. The back is clear plastic. Inside are gum and a toy. The toy in this container is a paper figure of a girl on a plastic stand.

TV Dinner

Category: Food items
Contents: Gum and candy, 0.9 oz.
Size: 3"h, $4\frac{5}{16}$"w, $\frac{5}{8}$"d
Made for: Concord Confections Inc., Ontario, Canada
Made in: Canada
Value: $4.00 – 5.50
Description: Container shaped like frozen TV dinner. Box made of paper. Inside is plastic TV dinner-like tray. Seal reads "Ready to peel & serve."

Tamagotchi

Category: Miscellaneous
Contents: Candy pastel eggs, 0.3 oz.
Size: $2\frac{5}{16}$"h, $1\frac{7}{8}$"w, $1\frac{5}{16}$"d
Made for: Creative Confection Concepts Inc., Milwaukee, WI 53209
Made in: China
Cost new: $1.87 \ **Value:** $4.00 – 5.00
Description: Came in many colors. Has a chain and loop attached to a ring on top. Label says "Reward yourself with Tamagotchi Treats! Feed Me!" © 1997.

Tanks

Category: Transportation
Contents: Small balls wrapped in plastic
Size: $1\frac{1}{4}$"h, $\frac{7}{8}$"w, $2\frac{1}{8}$"d
Made for: R.L. Albert & Son Inc., New York, NY 10457
Made in: Japan and Philippines
Value: $7.50 – 10.00
Description: Other than color, these two tanks are virtually identical but made in different countries, Japan and the Philippines. Embossed on the bottom of one tank: "© SLK 74 NEW YORK made in PHILIPPINES."

Tasmanian Devil

Category: Gumball dispensers
Contents: Gumballs
Size: $3\frac{1}{4}$"h, $2\frac{1}{4}$"w, $1\frac{3}{4}$"d
Made for: Processed Plastic Co., Montgomery, IL 60538
Made in: China (gum in Canada, assembled in U.S.A.)
Value: $3.50 – 5.50
Description: A Tim Mee Toy, © 1989. Taz stands next to a block of wood with hands around it. Lift Taz's arm to dispense gumballs. Embossed on the back: "Processed Plastic Co. Montgomery, IL. ™& © 1989 Warner Bros., Inc."

Tasmanian Devil (Jawbreaker)

Category: Characters
Contents: Jaw breaker, 4.5 oz.
Size: 3⅛"h, 2½"w, 2¼"d
Made for: Creative Confection Concepts, Milwaukee, WI 53209
Made in: Mexico
Cost new: $2.29 \ **Value:** $6.00 – 8.00
Description: Inside of the tag reads "14 days to make, 7 days to eat. The biggest, longest-lasting lip-smacking Jawbreaker in America." Came with a plastic carrying cord. Embossed on the bottom: "Made in Mexico ™& © 1996 WARNER BROS."

Tauntauns (head)

Category: Characters
Contents: Colored candy pellets, 0.5 oz.
Size: 2⁵⁄₁₆"h, 2¹¹⁄₁₆"w, 2¾"d
Made for: Topps Co., Duryea, PA 18642
Made in: Hong Kong
Value: $6.50 – 8.00
Description: Part of "The Empire Strikes Back" container series. To get candy out, turn closure to hole in the container. Embossed on side of the head: "© 1980 LFL."

Telephone (15 buttons)

Category: Telephones
Contents: Gum, 20g
Size: 3⁹⁄₁₆"h, 1⅛"w, ⅞"d
Made for: Nueva Marve
Made in: Mexico
Cost new: $0.45 \ **Value:** $2.00 – 2.50
Description: Sticker on the back reads: "Elaborado por: Nueba Marve Ingredientes etc. Contenido Nato 20 g Reg. S. S. A. No. 117981 A Enriqueta 3236 Col. Bondojito C. P. 07850 Hecho En Mexico Tel. 751-49-88 893-12-44."

Telephone (Call Me)

Category: Telephones
Contents: Gum, 0.53 oz.
Size: 4⅜"h, 1⅜"w, ⅝"d
Made for: Goodlite Products Inc., Bedford, TX 76021
Made in: China
Value: $3.00 – 4.00
Description: Screw-on closure is where antenna would be. Front flips open to expose buttons for dialing. Embossed on the front: "© 1994 JYCO CHINA."

Telephone (Candy Caller)

Category: Telephones
Contents: Smarties, 2.5 oz.
Size: 8¼"h, 2⅜"w, 1⁵⁄₁₆"d
Made for: BerZerk Candy Werks, Memphis, TN 38119
Made in: China
Value: $5.50 – 6.50
Description: Has antenna that rises more than two inches. Battery-operated sound when any of nine buttons are pushed. Paper label on the front reads "This phone and all the candy inside belongs to _____ name. And Candy Caller."

Telephone (cellular)

Category: Telephones
Contents: Gum, 1.24 oz.
Size: 6⅜"h, 1¼"w, ¾"d
Made for: Amurol Products Co., Naperville, IL 60567-2286
Made in: U.S.A.
Value: $4.00 – 5.00
Description: Toy phone is filled with bubble gum. Embossed on the back: "Made In China."

Telephone (center antenna)

Category: Telephones
Contents: Gum, 20g
Size: 4¼"h, 1¹⁄₁₆"w, ⅞"d
Made for: Nueva Marve, Mexico
Made in: Mexico
Cost new: $0.69 \ **Value:** $2.00 – 3.50
Description: Embossed on the front: "PHONE," with a backwards letter N. Push-in closure, on bottom. Label on the back reads "Elaborado Por: Nueva marve ingredientes: etc. Contenido neto 20 g. Reg. S.S.A. N 117981 !A Enriqueta 3236 Co."

Telephone (candy phone)

Category: Telephones
Contents: Gum 5, oz.
Size: 6¼"h, 3⅝"w, 3½"d
Made for: The Jelly Bean Factory, Cincinnati, OH 45227
Made in: China
Cost new: $2.99 \ **Value:** $5.00 – 6.50
Description: Back label reads "Candy Phone filled with bubble gum." Can also be used as bank. This telephone also comes as Easter Phone and is distributed by The Dayton Hudson Corp., Minn., MN 55402.

Telephone (E. Rosen)

Category: Telephones
Contents: Colored candy beads, 1 oz.
Size: 1⅞"h, 4¼"w, 1¹³⁄₁₆"d
Made for: E. Rosen Company, Pawtucket, RI 02860
Made in: Hong Kong
Cost new: $0.29 \ **Value:** $15.00 – 20.00
Description: On the bottom is the closure and "Made in Hong Kong." The dial and hand set moves. Sold at Woolworth 5 – 10.

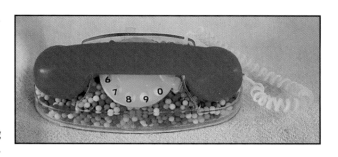

Telephone (flip phone)

Category: Telephones
Contents: Gum, 1.26 oz.
Size: 6⅜"h (antenna in), 2⅜"w, 1¼"d
Made for: Leaf Inc., Lake Forest, IL 60045
Made in: China
Cost new: $1.19 \ **Value:** $4.00 – 6.00
Description: Front opens with buttons to press. Buttons play different sounds. Has red light above No. 1. Antenna pulls out. Front label reads "Rain-blo, Flip Phone, bubble gum, try me." Closure on the back. Embossed on the inside front cover: "EMS Marketing, San Diego, CA 92120."

Telephone (Phoney Candy)

Category: Telephones
Contents: Candy, 0.35 oz.
Size: 2¾"h, 1¼"w, 1¹⁄₁₆"d
Made for: Fleer Corp., Philadelphia, PA 19141
Made in: U.S.A.
Value: $8.00 – 10.00
Description: Embossed on the front: "Phoney Candy." Has raised dial, money return, and door with keyhole. Embossed on the door: "NET WT. .35 oz." Candy has writing on it, including, "Call me," "911," and "I'm busy."

Telephone (Space Phone)

Category: Telephones
Contents: Smarties, 2⅜ oz.
Size: 2¹³⁄₁₆"h, 4¹⁄₁₆"w, 8"d
Made for: Hilco Corp., Norristown, PA 19401
Made in: Taiwan
Value: $7.00 – 8.50
Description: Has nine white buttons with green numbers. Battery-operated to make sounds. Embossed on the bottom: "Made In Taiwan."

Telephone Booth (English)

Category: Nonplastic
Contents: English toffee, 7.05 oz.
Size: 7"h, 3"w, 3"d
Made for: Churchill's Confectionery, U.K. and U.S.A.
Made in: England
Cost new: $5.97 \ **Value:** $7.00 – 8.00
Description: All tin. Doubles as a bank. Came with plastic cover taped on top as a seal. Boy is waiting outside the booth and girl is trying to reach the phone's coin slot. On back is a dog on his hind feet, looking at a butterfly. The sides show girl from left and right. Boy, dog, and windows are raised. On the bottom: "Churchill's Heritage of England Telephone Kiosk (Money Box)." Registered design by Allan Bodnitz.

Thumb

Category: Miscellaneous
Contents: Gum, 1.7 oz.
Size: 3¾"h, 1¾"w, 1⅝"d
Made for: Creative Confection Concepts, Milwaukee, WI 53209
Made in: Mexico
Cost new: $1.19 \ **Value:** $6.00 – 8.00
Description: Tag tied with a plastic cord that reads "Bubble Thumb Gum." Thumbprint is really face of a laughing person. Came with a carrying cord.

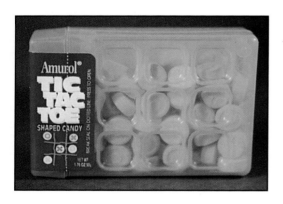

Tic Tac Toe

Category: Games
Contents: Colored pressed candy, 1.76 oz.
Size: 3⁹⁄₁₆"h, 2⅜"w, 1"d
Made for: Amurol Confections Co., Yorkville, IL 60560
Made in: U.S.A.
Cost new: $0.97 \ **Value:** $3.00 – 4.00
Description: Candy has "X"s and "O"s embossed on it. Box indented with nine squares for use as a game board. Flip-top closure.

Tin (girl's picture)

Category: Nonplastic
Contents: Jasmine flavored cachous candy
Size: ⅞"h, 1¹¹⁄₁₆"w
Made for: Christopher Brookes Fords, Seattle, WA 98125
Made in: England
Value: $2.00 – 3.00
Description: This small round tin comes with a plastic insert inside. Paper label on the back.

Tongue (Bubble Tongue)

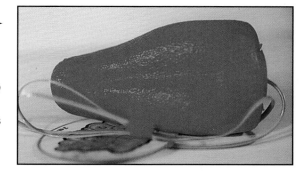

Category: Miscellaneous
Contents: Gum, 2 oz.
Size: 3⅞"h, 2⅛"w, 1⅛"d
Made for: Creative Confection Concepts Inc., Milwaukee, WI 53209
Cost new: $1.47 \ **Value:** $5.50 – 7.50
Description: No markings on the container. Top side of the tongue is rough, bottom side smooth. Has a plastic carrying cord.

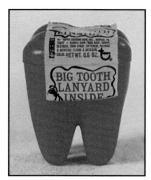

Tooth (Big Tooth)

Category: Miscellaneous
Contents: Gum, 0.6 oz.
Size: 2¼"h, 1¾"w, 1½"d
Made for: Topps Chewing Gum Inc., Duryea, PA 18642
Value: $6.00 – 8.00
Description: Label reads "Big Tooth, Lanyard Inside."

Tooth (T-Rex)

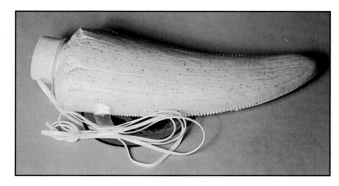

Category: Animals
Contents: Bubble gum, 1.5 oz.
Size: 6¼"h, 2¼"w, 1½"d
Made for: Creative Confection Concepts, Milwaukee, WI 53209
Made in: Mexico
Cost new: $1.29 \ **Value:** $8.00 – 10.00
Description: Tooth has serrated edges and crack on both sides. Screw-top closure with protective seal. Came with a plastic lacing. Tag has picture of a T-Rex.

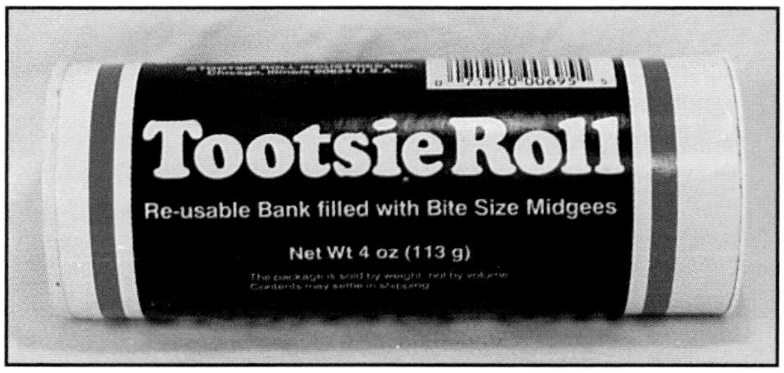

Tootsie Roll

Category: Food items
Contents: Bite-sized Tootsie Rolls, 4 oz.
Size: 5⅞"h, 2⅜"d
Made for: Tootsie Roll Industries, Chicago, IL 60629
Value: $2.00 – 3.00
Description: Looks like a big Tootsie Roll. Has coin slot for use as a bank. Written on the side: "Tootsie Roll Re-usable Bank." Container made of cardboard tube with plastic on one end and tin on the other.

Top

Category: Miscellaneous
Contents: Powder candy
Size: 2"h, 1⅜"w
Cost new: $0.30 \ **Value:** $3.00 – 5.00
Description: Purchased in Yuma, Arizona, in 1996. No label or markings. Filled with candy resembling brown sugar.

Top (Candy Invader)

Category: Games
Contents: Gum
Size: 4"h, 3¼"w
Made for: Bee International, Chula Vista, CA 91912
Made in: China
Value: $6.00 – 8.00
Description: This container is a real top. Twist lower part and push top button and the alien drops and spins. Embossed under ship's lip is "U.S. Patent Pending – Made in China." It has U.F.O. on the front and a picture of an alien's head and the word "EXIT" on the back door.

Top (Fantastic Four)

Category: Characters
Contents: Gum, 2 oz.
Size: 4³⁄₁₆"h, 3"w
Made for: Classic Heroes Inc., Stuart, FL 34995
Made in: China
Value: $5.00 – 7.50
Description: Part of the Classic Heroes collection of container tops. This is a member of the Fantastic Four. Item No. 62000. Label reads "™ & © 1995 Classic Heroes, Inc. All rights reserved. Marvel Characters."

Top (Iron Man)

Category: Characters
Contents: Gum, 2 oz.
Size: 4¼"h, 3"w
Made for: Classic Heroes Inc., Stuart, FL 34995
Made in: China
Value: $5.00 – 7.50
Description: Part of series of Classic Heroes containers. This is Iron Man. Tamper seal at base. Label on the back reads "™ & © 1995 Classic Heroes, Inc. All rights reserved. Marvel Characters." Item No. 62000.

Top (spinning top)

Category: Games
Contents: Merry Mix, 1.8 oz.
Size: 6⅞"h, 2⅝"w
Made for: The Jelly Bean Factory, Cincinnati, OH 45227
Made in: China
Cost new: $2.99 \ **Value:** $5.00 – 6.00
Description: Front label reads "Musical Spinning Top, with blinking lights. © 1997 Willie Wonka's MERRY MIX™· Toy made in China, candy made in U.S.A." Back label: "To re-launch: 1. Press top button to ensure bottom peg on body of zing zong is fully extended. 2. Insert bottom peg into the hole of the spinning top. 3. Twist spinning top slowly until tightened (not more than 5 times). 4. Press top button to launch the spinning top. (Spinning top should be launched no higher than 24" off the ground.)"

Top (Wolverine)

Category: Characters
Contents: Gum, 2 oz.
Size: 4⅝"h, 3"w
Made for: Classic Heroes Inc., Stuart, FL 34995
Made in: China
Value: $5.00 – 7.50
Description: Top features Wolverine of the X-Men. To open, break tamper-evident seal at base of figure. Label reads "™ & © 1995 Classic Heroes, Inc. All rights reserved. Marvel Characters."

Toxic Crusader (Big Nose)

Category: Characters
Contents: Colored candy tablets, 0.4oz.
Size: 2³⁄₁₆"h, 1½"w, 2½"d
Made for: Topps Co., Duryea, PA 18642
Made in: China
Value: $6.00 – 7.50
Description: Part of Toxic Crusader series. Features head of Big Nose. Embossed on the bottom: "© 1991 TROMA, INC."

Toxic Crusader (Greenhat)

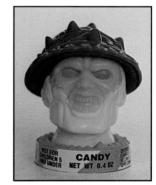

Category: Characters
Contents: Colored candy tablets, 0.4 oz.
Size: 2⅜"h, 1⅞"w, 1¾"d
Made for: Topps Co., Duryea, PA 18642
Made in: China
Value: $6.00 – 7.50
Description: Head only. Embossed on the bottom: "© 1991 TROMA, INC."

Toxic Crusader (Mask)

Category: Characters
Contents: Colored candy tablets, 0.4 oz.
Size: 2½"h, 1¾"w, 1¾"d
Made for: Topps Co., Duryea, PA 18642
Made in: China
Value: $6.00 – 7.50
Description: Part of Toxic Crusader series. Head only. Embossed on the bottom: "© 1991 TROMA, INC."

Toxic Crusader (Pop Eye)

Category: Characters
Contents: Colored candy tablets, 0.4 oz.
Size: 2⅛"h, 1¾"w, 1⅝"d
Made for: Topps Co., Duryea, PA 18642
Made in: China
Value: $6.00 – 7.50
Description: Part of a series of Toxic Crusader containers. This is Pop Eye. Embossed on the bottom: "© 1991 TROMA, INC."

Treasure Chest

Category: Miscellaneous
Contents: Assorted candy, 5 oz.
Size: 2¹⁵⁄₁₆"h, 4⅜"w, 3⅝"d
Made for: Galene Au Chocolat®, Cincinnati, OH 45227
Made in: China
Cost new: $4.99 \ **Value:** $6.00 – 7.50
Description: Chest has padlock and a key hanging on the front. Moveable handle.

Tree (Christmas Tree Necklace)

Category: Holidays
Contents: Runts Merry Mix candy, 0.35 oz.
Size: 2½"h, 2⅛"w, 1⅛"d
Made for: Dayton Hudson, Minneapolis, MN 55402
Made in: Mexico
Cost new: $0.99 \ **Value:** $3.00 – 4.00
Description: Comes with a red plastic cord. Card attached reads "Christmas Tree Necklace."

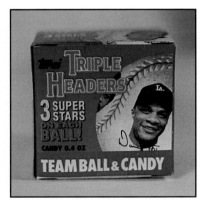

Triple Headers

Category: Nonplastic
Contents: Candy, 0.4 oz, ball & stand
Size: 2"h, 2"w, 2"d
Made for: Topps Co., Duryea, PA 18642
Made in: China
Value: $3.00 – 5.00
Description: Made out of paper. Twenty-six in the series. Box contains baseball and candy. © 1992.

Troll

Category: Characters
Contents: Candy, 0.25 oz.
Size: 2¹⁵⁄₁₆"h (excluding hair), 2¹⁄₁₆"w, 1⁹⁄₁₆"d
Made for: Topps Co., Duryea, PA 18642
Made in: China
Value: $4.00 – 5.00
Description: Series of troll containers © 1992. Came with different color hair. Closure is on the bottom, under feet. Embossed on the back of left leg: "© The Topps Company Inc."

Trolly Car

Category: Transportation
Contents: Colored candy beads, 0.6 oz.
Size: 2³⁄₁₆"h, 1⁵⁄₁₆"w, 3³⁄₁₆"d
Made for: Allen Mitchell Products, Oxnard, CA 93030
Made in: Hong Kong
Value: $12.00 – 15.00
Description: Embossed on the bottom is the Allen Mitchell star and "Made in Hong Kong." It has a paper label on each side reading "TROLLY CAR."

Truck (Box)

Category: Transportation
Contents: Colored candy beads, 1 oz.
Size: 1⅞"h, 1½"w, 3⅞"d
Made for: E. Rosen Company, Pawtucket, RI 02862
Cost new: $0.29 \ **Value:** $12.00 – 15.00
Description: This candy container comes boxed with the top cover only with plastic wrap so you can see the toy. It is part of a Candy Box series. The box has "candy-filled TOY TRUCK" printed on it.

Truck (Jelly Belly)

Category: Transportation
Contents: Jelly Belly sours, 6 oz.
Size: 3⅛"h, 1¹⁵⁄₁₆"w, 5¹¹⁄₁₆"d
Made for: Goelitz Confectionery Co., Chicago, IL 60064
Cost new: $8.50 \ **Value:** $9.00 – 10.50
Description: Container came wrapped in clear plastic, with cardboard label that the truck rests on. Back doors open.

Truck (See's)

Category: Nonplastic
Contents: Chocolate eggs and suckers
Size: 4⅝"h, 10"w, 3½"d
Made for: See's Candy Shop Inc., Los Angeles, CA
Made in: U.S.A.
Cost new: $12.00 \ **Value:** $12.00 – 15.00
Description: Body made of tin; frame and wheels made of plastic. Embossed on the bottom: "STK #3605 The ERTL CO. Dyersville, Iowa 52040 Made In U.S.A." Back doors open. Wheels turn.

Tube (Slimer, Ghostbusters)

Category: Miscellaneous
Contents: Bubble gum, 1.6 oz.
Size: 5⅝"h, 1½"w, 1"d
Made for: Amurol Products Co., Naperville IL 60566
Value: $8.00 – 10.00
Description: Container looks like a tooth paste tube. The Real Ghostbusters™ Slimer™ © 1984 Columbia Pictures Industries, Inc. © 1986 CPT Holdings, Inc. All rights reserved.

Turtle (on wheels)

Category: Animals
Contents: Colored candy balls
Size: 1¼"h, 2¾"w, 4"d
Made in: Hong Kong
Cost new: $1.29 \ **Value:** $10.00 – 15.00
Description: Push turtle and the head and tail move in and out.

Tweety

Category: Gumball dispensers
Contents: Gumballs
Size: 3¼"h, 1¾"w
Made for: Processed Plastic Co., Montgomery, IL 60538
Made in: China
Value: $5.50 – 7.00
Description: A Tim Mee Toy from 1995. Tweety is sitting on a birdcage. Item No. 26000. To open, break tamper-evident seal at base of figure. Cage has door that opens.

Tweety (bank)

Category: Characters
Contents: Gum 5.3 oz.
Size: 4¾"h, 4⅛"w, 4⁵⁄₁₆"d
Made for: Creative Confection Concepts, Milwaukee, WI 53209
Made in: China
Cost new: $4.99 \ **Value:** $8.00 – 12.00
Description: Tweety Bird container doubles as a bank. Push-in closure. Embossed on the bottom: "Made in China, ™ & © 1997 Warner Bros."

Two Face (bust)

Category: Characters
Contents: Gum, 0.4 oz.
Size: 2¼"h, 2³⁄₁₆"w, 1³⁄₁₆"d
Made for: Topps Co., Duryea, PA 18642
Made in: China
Cost new: $0.97 \ **Value:** $3.50 – 5.50
Description: Batman's nemesis. Right side of Two Face is black except his face. Left side is violet, with white hair. Embossed on right shoulder: "™ & © DC COMICS 1995."

U.F.O.

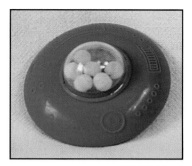

Category: Transportation
Contents: Pressed colored candy
Size: 1¼"h, 3½"w
Made for: Tapper Candy Inc., Cleveland, OH 44128
Made in: China
Cost new: $1.97 \ **Value:** $3.00 – 4.00
Description: Comes as party favors in a package of six. On the front of the package:
"THE ORIGINAL – Candy – PARTY FAVORS™ – No. 46200 – 6 CANDY U.F.O's."

Umbrella (Rainbow)

Category: Miscellaneous
Contents: Colored candy balls
Size: 6"h, ¹³⁄₁₆"w
Made for: R.L. Albert & Son Inc., New York, NY 10457
Made in: Japan
Value: $7.00 – 9.00

Description: Umbrella is wrapped with a plastic label that reads: "Rainbow Umbrella."

Uncle Fester (Addams Family)

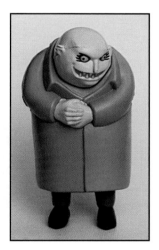

Category: Characters
Contents: Pressed candy in skull-and-bones shapes, 0.28 oz.
Size: 4⅛"h, 2¼"w, 2"d
Made for: Bee International, Chula Vista, CA 91912
Made in: China
Value: $6.00 – 7.00
Description: Uncle Fester from the Addams Family. Embossed on the back: "© 1993 HBPC."

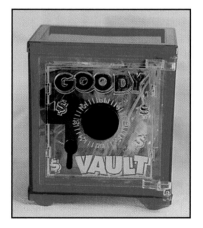

Vault (Goody)

Category: Miscellaneous
Contents: Candy and toys
Size: 5¹⁄₁₆"h, 4¼"w, 3⅜"d
Made for: Trapper Candies Inc., Cleveland, OH 44128
Made in: China
Value: $5.00 – 7.00
Description: It comes in a box and it has its own secret combination. Inside the vault are candy and toys. This one has Tootsie Roll Pop and SweetTarts for candy and eye glasses, dice, bugs, finger tip, and play money. Has a slit on the top for use as a bank.

Volkswagen (toy car)

Category: Transportation
Contents: Tart 'N' Tangy, 2.5 oz.
Size: 2¹³⁄₁₆"h, 2⅞"w, 4¹⁵⁄₁₆"d
Made for: The Jelly Bean Factory, Cincinnati, OH 45227
Made in: China
Cost new: $1.97 \ **Value:** $3.00 – 5.00
Description: Has paper-covered bumpers with hearts on the ends, license plate that reads "LUV," and sticker of a bear as the driver. Also a bank. White spoke wheels. Came in different colors and stickers.

Wakko (Animaniacs)

Category: Characters
Contents: Gum, 0.4 oz.
Size: 2⅜"h, 2½"w, 2⅜"d
Made for: Topps Co., Duryea, PA 18642
Made in: China
Value: $5.00 – 6.00
Description: From the Animaniacs cartoon. Head only. Embossed on the back: "™& © Warner Bros."

Wand (Magic)

Category: Miscellaneous
Contents: Candy stars
Size: 12¾"h, 2⅞"w, 1½"d
Made for: Candy Containers & More Inc., Oxnard, CA 93030
Made in: China
Cost new: $0.79 \ **Value:** $5.00 – 7.00
Description: The closure is a red plug with a star embossed on it. Sold in a plastic bag with a card on top that reads "Candy Filled Magic Wand. Net Wt. 1.32-oz. (35g)."

Watches (candy)

Category: Miscellaneous
Contents: Candy in shape of fruit
Size: 1¹⁄₁₆"h, 7⅛"w, 1⁵⁄₁₆"d
Made for: Tapper Candy Inc., Cleveland, OH 44146
Made in: China
Cost new: $3.29 \ **Value:** $6.50 – 8.50
Description: It came on a card with four watches in it. The card reads "Candy Party Favors, 4 Candy Watches." Net Wt. of candy 0.88 oz.

Water Bottle

Category: Bottles and jars
Contents: Tart candy rolls, 5.5 oz.
Size: 6½"h, 3¾"w, 3⁵⁄₁₆"d
Made for: The Jelly Bean Factory, Fairfax, OH 45227
Made in: China
Cost new: $2.99 \ **Value:** $4.00 – 5.00
Description: This is a working water bottle after the candy is removed. © GAC 1997. Comes with a detachable shoulder strap.

Watermelon Kid

Category: Food items
Contents: Gum, 1.7 oz.
Size: 4⅝"h, 2⅛"w, 1⅜"d
Made for: Creative Confection Concepts, Milwaukee, WI 53209
Made in: Mexico
Cost new: $1.19 \ **Value:** $8.00 – 10.00
Description: Label reads: "The Watermelon Kids! You can eat the seeds!" Contains watermelon bubble gum. Has a plastic carrying cord.

Witch

Category: Characters
Contents: Candy
Size: 3"h, 1½"w, 1⁹⁄₁₆"d
Made for: Ce De Candy, Inc., Union, NJ 07083
Value: $5.50 – 7.00
Description: Has a screw-on closure with ring for hanging. Inside of the cap is "31."

Witch with Broom

Category: Characters
Contents: Colored candy beads, ¾ oz.
Size: 4"h, 1⅜"w, 1½"d
Made for: E. Rosen Company, Pawtucket, RI 02860
Made in: Hong Kong
Value: $7.00 – 8.00
Description: The head is the closure. The witch is holding a broom with two hands. Hong Kong embossed on the bottom.

Woody & Bull's Eye (Toy Story 2)

Category: Characters
Contents: Nerds
Size: 8"h, 4¾"w, 3³⁄₁₆"d
Made for: McDonald's Corp., Oak Brook, IL 60521
Made in: China
Cost new: $2.50 \ **Value:** $3.00 – 5.00
Description: Embossed on the bottom is "Mfg. for McD Corp. China/Chine HK 06 © 1999 McDonald's Corp. © Disney/Pixar – Disney/Pixar Toy Story 2." Candy Net Wt. 1.5 oz. The candy is deposited in the bottom and you push down on the top of the base to collapse bull's eye and dispense candy. One in a series of six.

Wrist Watch

Category: Miscellaneous
Contents: Colored candy beads
Size: 7/8"h 2 3/8"w 2"d
Made for: Bee Distributing, Los Angeles, CA
Made in: Hong Kong
Value: $12.00 – 15.00

Description: The face of the watch is made so that if you move it the time will change. It came with a ring around the watchband. The candy in inside the band witch in a plastic tube that measures 5½" in length if stretched out. On back on the watch is embossed "Hong Kong." The sticker label reads "ING.SUGAR ART.FLAV.U.S. CERT. COL. MADE IN HONG KONG FOR BEE DISTRIBUTING, LOS ANGELES CALIF."

Wrist Wrap

Category: Miscellaneous
Contents: Jaw breakers, 1 oz.
Size: 2½"h, 3½"w, 1¼"d
Made for: Creative Confection Concepts, Milwaukee, WI 53209
Made in: Mexico
Cost new: $1.29 \ **Value:** $2.50 – 4.00
Description: Label says, "Candy on the Go!" Vinyl pouch for wearing on the wrist.

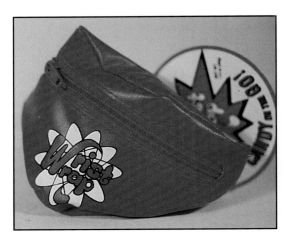

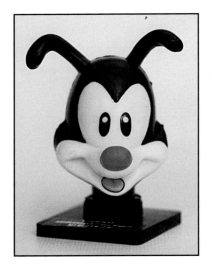

Yakko (Animanics)

Category: Characters
Contents: Gum, 0.4 oz.
Size: 2 5/8"h, 1 7/8"w, 1½"d
Made for: Topps Co., Duryea, PA 18642
Made in: China
Value: $5.00 – 6.00
Description: Head only. From the Animaniacs cartoon. Embossed on the back: "™ & © Warner Bros. © 1995."

Yoda (Europe)

Category: Characters
Contents: Candy Star Wars characters
Size: 1 13/16"h, 3 1/8"w, 1½"d
Made for: Topps Ireland Ltd., Ballincollig Co.
Made in: China
Value: $5.00 – 6.50
Description: This Star Wars candy containers was only released in Europe. It comes in a bag with a trading card.

Yoda (head)

Category: Characters
Contents: Colored candy pellets, 0.5 oz.
Size: 2⅛"h, 2⁷⁄₁₆"w, 1½"d
Made for: The Topps Co., Duryea, PA 18642
Made in: Hong Kong
Value: $6.50 – 8.50
Description: Part of a series of The Empire Strikes Back containers. To get candy out, turn closure to the hole in container. Embossed on back of the head: © 1980 LFL.

Yoyo

Category: Games
Contents: Tart 'N' Tinys candy, 1.3oz.
Size: 2¼"w, 2"d
Made for: Imperial Toy Corp., Los Angeles, CA 90021
Made in: China
Value: $4.50 – 6.00
Description: Yoyo doubles as container. "Candy Club" embossed on both ends. Front label reads: "Yummy Yoyo – Filled With Candy Coated Willy Wonka's Tart 'n Tinys – Great For Tricks." Candy removed by inserting a coin between words Candy and Club, then unscrewing plug. © 1996. Also comes on a small card #4663.

Yoyo (CE)

Category: Games
Contents: Candy
Size: 2⅜"h, 1⅝"w
Made for: Cap Toys Inc., Bedford Hills, OH 44146
Made in: Korea
Value: $4.50 – 6.00
Description: This is a useable toy. Candy is colored beads. Net wt. 20g. It has a closure on each side.

Yoyo (Mexican)

Category: Games
Contents: Gum
Size: 1¾"h, 1³⁄₁₆"w
Made for: Candies Tolteca Co, Mexican Candy, Fresno, CA 93744
Made in: Mexico
Cost new: $1.19 \ **Value:** $2.00 – 3.50
Description: You can see gum on both sides. Comes with a small string.